W9-BEB-815

THE PLAYER

THE PLAYER

CHRISTY MATHEWSON, BASEBALL, AND THE AMERICAN CENTURY

Philip Seib

FOUR WALLS EIGHT WINDOWS
New York / London

Published in the United States by

Four Walls Eight Windows
39 West 14th Street
New York, NY 10011

U.K. offices:
Four Walls Eight Windows/Turnaround
Unit 3, Olympia Trading Estate
Coburg Road, Wood Green
London N22 6TZ, England

http://www.4w8w.com

First printing September 2003.

Library of Congress Cataloging-in-Publication Data

Seib, Philip M., 1949–
        The player : Christy Mathewson, baseball, and the American century / Philip Seib.
            p.   cm.
        Includes bibliographical references and index.
        ISBN 1-56858-268-4
        1. Mathewson, Christy, 1880–1925. 2. Baseball players—United States—Biography. I. Title.
        GV865.M37S45 2003
        796.357'092—dc21   2003052472

Book design by Terry Bain

10 9 8 7 6 5 4 3 2 1

Printed in Canada

For the real Christy

Contents

Preface

I love to sit in a ballpark and let the rhythms of baseball push me back into the past as I like to remember it. Even in the new stadiums with motorized roofs, my memory pulls up sandlot afternoons and twenty-five-cent hot dogs. Down on the field, the stately progress of the game remains nicely archaic. The ballpark is one of the few places in today's world where the past need not retreat.

I think there is substance to the idea that understanding baseball is helpful in understanding America. This is not just a matter of knowing how to keep score or how to throw a changeup. Rather, it involves following the interwoven threads of baseball and American politics and culture and seeing how they join in a seamless fabric.

Over the years, a few ballplayers have influenced much more than the game itself, becoming important symbols and social forces. Jackie Robinson is a good example. His story has been told many times and his role in sport and nation is well established. Other players have also profoundly influenced both baseball and national life but have received far less attention. Among them Christy Mathewson stands out.

He transformed and transcended the game, with achievements on the diamond that are unmatched to this day, and with accomplishments off the field that made him one of the best-known Americans of his time. He defined athletic and moral excellence, bridging sport and national culture.

Almost ninety years have passed since Mathewson last pitched, and although baseball aficionados may know the statistics of his Hall of Fame career, time has blurred the larger picture of his life. Mathewson led professional baseball into the American mainstream, bringing rigorous personal standards to a game that had been best known for its players' boorish behavior on and off the field. He pitched with grit and grace, and he quickly became a hero to fans, a role model for children and a lasting symbol of sportsmanship. He was an important force in making baseball the only professional sport that mattered for many years.

I was drawn to his story partly because today sportsmanship is becoming obsolete, replaced by taunting, showboating and worse. Being a sports star used to be accompanied by a sense of responsibility to team and fans, but many of today's athletes don't want to be role models, unless it is part of a deal negotiated by their agents. That's a shame. We could use some more heroes, on the playing field and elsewhere.

There have been other great players, but Mathewson stands out because of the way his own life moved apace with the life of the country. During the first years of the twentieth century, Theodore Roosevelt was proclaiming the virtues of "the strenuous life," and Mathewson was a striking example of the blending of physical and moral strength. When celebrity culture took root, Mathewson jumped in, performing in vaudeville and films, endorsing products, writing popular fiction and otherwise capitalizing on his baseball fame. A few years later, while Woodrow Wilson was championing the politics of idealism, Mathewson tried to rid baseball of corruption that threatened the heart of the game. He also joined the army to fight a war that Wilson defined as a moral crusade. And after he was stricken with tuberculosis, Mathewson showed that his courage could reach an even higher plane.

At the outset of the American century, as the United States defined and asserted itself, Mathewson was always there. He was more than a baseball player—he was the quintessential new American hero, skilled and successful, ready to lead.

I found plenty of intriguing characters in Mathewson's baseball circle. John McGraw was a brilliant manager who transformed Mathewson from just another promising player into the game's greatest star. McGraw's belligerence on the field offered a striking contrast to Mathewson's unshakable dignity. Rube Marquard was instructed to model himself after Mathewson, but did so only while pitching. After leaving the ballpark, he cut a wide swath through New York's nightlife and reveled in scandal. The unscrupulous Hal Chase cared only about enriching himself and used any means available to do so. He was bitterly happy to be Mathewson's longtime foil. Sportswriters such as Ring Lardner and Grantland Rice were especially powerful in the era when words, not television images, told sports stories. They helped build the Mathewson legend.

Examining the connections between Mathewson's life and the life of the nation meant going beyond the domain of ballplayers. As I roamed, I encountered men and women who don't often show up in baseball biographies—Jane Addams, Edith Wharton, Dr. Edward Trudeau, Booth Tarkington and many others. I also found intriguing personal baseball histories of people such as Woodrow Wilson and Billy Sunday.

In the midst of this diverse crowd, Mathewson himself proved to be a somewhat elusive subject. Although he did not regret being a public figure, he was unfailingly discreet and protective of his privacy. There is no trail of stories comparable to those Babe Ruth left in his wake. But this lack of flamboyance was an important part of the Mathewson persona. He had faith in his values, and like his accomplishments on the diamond, they did not need flashy enhancement.

Christy Mathewson was a remarkable guy. In baseball and in wider realms of American life, he was a transforming presence—the consummate player. Understanding him and the game he played will take anyone a long way toward understanding America.

PROLOGUE

October 8, 1925

As the second game of the World Series was about to begin, quiet settled over Pittsburgh's Forbes Field.

Pittsburgh and Washington players, with mourning bands hastily sewn onto their uniforms, marched to center field, where the flag was lowered to half-staff. Forty-eight thousand people rose without a word, and tears began to flow.

Matty was gone.

He had died the previous evening. Tuberculosis killed him at age forty-five. He had not played for almost a decade, but no one had forgotten Christy Mathewson.

This was not just the passing of an athlete—it marked the end of the time when baseball became a truly national pastime and when players were first seen as heroes.

Throughout the country, newspaper tributes explained why Mathewson had meant so much to so many.

> Christy Mathewson owed his place in the hearts of his vast public less to the wizardry of his pitching arm than to the fact that he was a gentleman, a sportsman of the finest sort.
> —*Manchester (CT) Herald*

> While Mathewson's record in baseball will stand while the game lasts, it was not his prowess as an athlete that made him the idol of

American manhood, young and old. It was the character of the man. . . . He played for all that was in him, he fought the good fight and the clean fight. He was the incarnation of all those virtues with which we endow the ideal American.   —*New York Herald-Tribune*

This is the type of man who makes baseball worthy of its fame as the national game. The life of Christy Mathewson helped extend through the land the ideal of sportsmanship at its best, whether on the playing field or in the daily grind of human duty. As such, it helped build the nation.   —*Boston Transcript*

Christy Mathewson mirrored and influenced the changing character of America. His story and the story of his country flow together.

ONE

Playing for Fun

THE HOLE IN THE BARN wall wasn't much wider than the ball in the boy's hand. He reached back and threw as hard as he could. The ball shot through the hole. He picked up another ball and did it again . . . and again. In his mind's eye, he wasn't pitching in his backyard, but in a stadium filled with cheering people—cheering as he whipped his fastball past snarling batters. He fired one more ball through that little hole, into the hay stacked in the barn. The cheers grew louder.

Playing. That's what baseball is. Throw the ball, hit the ball, catch the ball. It's a game.

But it is also something more. The competition, graceful and intense, is presumed to be a window on the American spirit. Those who master the art of baseball preside over more than the field of play. They become cultural icons, reflecting the state of the nation and influencing the tenor of national life. Only a few players reach this level: Babe Ruth, Joe DiMaggio, Jackie Robinson, Hank Aaron, and Cal Ripken among them. Before them all was Christy Mathewson.

He was a gentleman in a ruffian's game, a sportsman among brawlers. He exemplified personal virtue as an American characteristic when the nation was defining its values. And he was enormously, dazzlingly talented at the game he loved.

On the days he was good—and most days he was very good—he

left batters frustrated, reaching for a pitch that suddenly wasn't there. The fastball shot by, the curve dipped out of reach and the mysterious fade-away broke in the wrong direction. Putting bat on ball is the hardest task in sports, and Mathewson made it even harder than usual. During his long career, not many opponents crossed home plate against him—barely two every nine innings. Any batter who did hit him solidly was unlikely to ever see the same pitch again.

Mathewson's temperament as well as his skill lifted the play of his teammates. Another player's fielding error or failure to drive in a run would not draw even a glare from him, much less a harsh word. One of his catchers, Chief Meyers, said: "How we loved to play for him! We'd break our necks for that guy."

And he started by just playing, out by the barn.

Factoryville, Pennsylvania, hasn't changed much since Christy grew up there in the 1880s and '90s. Houses from that time, including the ones he lived in, stand in the little valley about sixteen miles northwest of Scranton. Spacious porches look out over lawns running down to Tunkhannock Creek, where the fishing is good. The railroad tracks have been replaced by a not-very-busy state highway, and there's a stoplight at the corner where the road curves down the hill into the village. It's a pretty place, with brooks and farmers' fields close by.

The village was officially created in 1828 with the establishment of its first post office. The railroad brought salesmen and a few visitors to town, and jobs could be found at the tannery and the grist mill. Main Street featured a bank and a photography studio. In the 1880s, the population was about 640.

Christopher Mathewson was born August 12, 1880, in the second-floor bedroom of a trim white house on Main Street, now College Avenue. He was named after an uncle who had promised to bestow a thousand dollars upon a namesake. His parents, Gilbert and

Minerva, were of New England stock, and their families had settled in Pennsylvania as part of the movement west, searching for opportunity and elbow room.

The cotton goods factory that gave the town its name had failed, so Gilbert did some farming, like others in the town, and a bit of carpentry on the side. He didn't have to work too hard because Minerva was a Capwell, which meant a lot in Factoryville. Town records list a Capwell as one of the first physicians. A Capwell owned the first hotel, and he was succeeded in running it by a Mathewson. During Christy's childhood, Minerva's money ensured that the Mathewsons were always comfortable, if never wealthy.

Gilbert fought in the Civil War as a teenager and then landed a job in Washington, where he worked in the Senate post office. When he returned home, he presided over a family of three sons and two daughters. (Another boy died as an infant.)

With their family growing, the Mathewsons moved about a hundred yards down the street to a slightly larger house where Christy and his siblings would grow up. It was a comfortable, lively place. Minerva described it like this: "I've never had anything in my home too good to be used. I have always wanted my children to enjoy everything in it. A home is to live in. It's for your children and their friends."

The barn out back was nestled against a wooded hillside. Christy would practice pitching by himself, or recruit someone to play "hailey over," which involved arcing a throw over the barn to a catcher on the other side.

He went to grade school in Factoryville and enjoyed the idyllic life of small town America: fishing for pickerel in the Tunkhannock, playing trombone in the town band (which meant he got to wear a brass-buttoned uniform), helping out with the family vegetable garden, and playing ball. Christy later said that he had not been particularly precocious in baseball. While very young, he played the outfield or second base—anywhere the older boys told him to play. Everyone wanted to pitch; that was the position for heroes who would mow down enemy batters, and it was reserved for the oldest boys on the team.

Christy practiced pitching on his own, with a ball if one was handy or, more often, with stones. A cousin taught him how to make a stone curve in flight, and as Christy tramped through the woods around town, "I got to be a great stone thrower, and this practice increased my throwing power and taught me something about curves. When I was nine years old, I could throw a stone farther than any of the boys who were my chums."

Like many towns, Factoryville had its own amateur baseball team, made up of adults who took seriously their rivalries with neighboring villages. At age ten, Christy was made the team's "second catcher," a position that involved little more than fetching foul balls, carrying bats, and bringing water to the real players. Although proud to be associated even in this slight way with the team, he later recalled that the players were not perfect role models. Many "had whiskers on their faces and were really fat men."

He was eager to play ball at every opportunity. He later wrote, "I would rather play baseball than eat, and that is the spirit all boys need who expect to be good players." A cousin told a story about the time she hired Christy to pick strawberries in her yard. He worked hard until a ball game started. Using some of the money his cousin was paying him, Christy hired younger boys to finish the job so he could join the game.

His first chance to establish himself as a player came when he was fourteen. It was the day before a big game between Factoryville and Mill City, a despised rival seven miles away. Factoryville's pitcher became ill, and his usual backup was out of town. There was talk of sending for a semipro player and paying him to fill in, but the team didn't have the money for that.

"What about Christy?" someone asked. "The kid can pitch pretty well."

A tryout was arranged for the morning of the game, right in the middle of Main Street. In front of the Factoryville team and much of the rest of the town, Christy showed off his pitches and wrapped up his performance by striking out the captain. He had won himself the job. The team boarded its mule-drawn coach and headed for Mill City.

Here the storybook tale goes a bit awry. There was no pitching miracle on the Mill City diamond. After all, this was a fourteen-year-old throwing against adults. Christy gave up seventeen runs.

But the story has one more twist. For most of the game, Christy was as overmatched at the plate as he was in the pitcher's box. (There was as yet no mound for pitchers.) Each time he came to bat, he struck out . . . except once.

The bases were loaded, and Christy, swinging with the same cross-handed grip he used when hoeing potatoes, slashed at the ball and met it with all his weight. It soared over the left fielder's head, and three runs crossed the plate. Final score: Factoryville 19, Mill City 17. The boy was a hero.

This game was at the end of the summer, and soon it was time for Christy to return to school. There was no public high school in the area, but right down the street was Keystone Academy, a Baptist prep school whose founders included Christy's Grandmother Capwell. The school's articles of incorporation proclaim, "It shall be a literary institution for the education of the people in useful arts, sciences, and literature." The student handbook noted that "each day's work is begun by chapel exercise, consisting of singing, Scripture reading and prayer." By this time Christy's mother had decided that her son should become a Baptist preacher, and she saw Keystone as the perfect place for Christy to prepare for that career.

The campus consisted of twenty acres donated by the Capwells. The original red brick building stands on a leafy hill, with woods and fields stretching out behind it. Today, the campus covers 270 acres and the school has become a college, but it retains the quiet charm of the nineteenth century, with a string of nicely restored Victorian homes serving as a bridge between campus and town.

The 1898–1899 student handbook notes that "much attention is given to football and baseball. The physical part of our being is developed on the field while the mental is taken care of in the classrooms. . . . We believe in an amiable temper and aim to develop it while contesting for honors." At the end of the handbook's section about athletics is the name of the baseball team's captain, Christy Mathewson.

For a while at Keystone, Christy concentrated on football. He later said that while baseball might be the better spectator sport, football was more fun for the players. Nevertheless, he kept playing baseball, both for the school and in pickup games. His mother later recalled: "A good many times I've come out here and acted as umpire. . . . In those days, as now, no matter how excited the others got, they never could fuss Christy. He'd just stand aside while the others fought things out and at the end he'd say, 'Oh, come on and let's play ball.'"

While he was at Keystone, the Mill City team he had once defeated made him an extravagant offer: a dollar a game to pitch.

Christy later said, "It was such fun for me to play ball then that the idea of being paid for it struck me as finding money."

He had to get to the games on his own and bring his own catcher, so Christy would recruit one of his buddies and they'd walk the seven miles to the Mill City diamond along a tree-lined country road. Fred Brauer was one of those early catchers, and in later years he'd show his son his gnarled knuckles, the result of foul tips by batters who couldn't catch up with Christy's fastball. He never said if Christy split the dollar with him.

Christy played seven or eight times for Mill City, once pitching a shutout, which was a rare occurrence given the haphazard fielding of amateur ball in those days.

In the summer of 1898, just after graduating from Keystone, Christy took the train into Scranton to watch that city's YMCA team play Pittston. He sat in the stands, working his way through a five-cent bag of peanuts while waiting impatiently for the game to start. The Scranton pitcher did not show up that day, and one of the YMCA players who had seen Christy pitch walked over to the grandstand, nodded at the boy, and asked, "Want to work for us this afternoon?"

Christy scrambled into a uniform that was many sizes too big and started pitching. He struck out fifteen that day and was rewarded with an offer to come back and pitch regularly for Scranton. He would be paid enough to cover the cost of getting to and from Scranton and given a uniform that fit.

He also kept playing for Factoryville, and became a local celebrity, which did not impress his mother. She told of the day he was scheduled to pitch for his hometown against local rival Honesdale.

"There was a lot of practicing, so much that when the day came for the game Christy's potato patch had not been picked. I told him that he could not go to Honesdale unless the patch had been taken care of. On the morning of the game he tried to beg off. All of his teammates came to me. Without Christy, they said, Factoryville would be beaten by Honesdale. I answered that Factoryville would have to be beaten, then. There and then they saw a light, and every one of the nine pitched in and picked potatoes. They cleaned the field up before noon, I paid them with a good meal, and Factoryville won the game."

That victory over Honesdale led to Christy's best baseball deal to date. The Honesdale team offered him twenty dollars a month and board to play for them. "This seemed to me then a princely sum," he later said, "and I began to speak of 'J. P. Morgan and me.'"

Honesdale is about thirty miles east of Factoryville. The Honesdale Eagles played against teams from towns such as Goshen, Port Jervis, and Chester. On July 18, 1898, Christy pitched his first game for the Eagles, winning 16-7. A few days later, he pitched a 2-0 shutout, and on July 27 he pitched a seven-inning no-hitter against

Carbondale, winning 7-0. Over the course of the summer he won eight games for Honesdale.

The Honesdale Eagles were considered an amateur team, although today they would be called semipro. Players received small stipends, but they all held down other jobs or went to school. When a good prospect like Mathewson was noticed, the team would try to lure him away from wherever he was playing. Everyone was a free agent.

Games were played on unused farm fields or town lots like the Silk Mill Flats that the players cleared themselves. Teams might receive financial help from local businesses—sometimes cash, sometimes a keg of beer. Members of the community took fierce pride in their team and valued the bragging rights earned by victories over neighboring towns.

They also valued baseball itself. By the mid-nineteenth century, the game had become part of American culture, an enterprise that encouraged personal achievement and civic enthusiasm. Walt Whitman wrote: "I see great things in baseball. It's our game—the American game. It will take our people out of doors, fill them with oxygen, give them a larger physical stoicism. Tend to relieve us from being a nervous, dyspeptic set. Repair these losses, and be a blessing to us."

Most members of these teams played until their skills faded or their work and family responsibilities left them no time for the practices and games. Then they joined the ranks of the spectators as the next cadre of young men took their place.

Baseball had a huge following throughout the country, but that did not translate into support for the professional game. With few exceptions, baseball fans were more devoted to local amateur teams than to big league clubs. In 1890, the New York Giants drew only 60,000 fans for the entire season, total National League attendance was approximately 814,000, and the competing Players League attracted 979,000 fans. Few professional teams ever made a profit.

Amateur players considered themselves a more noble breed than the big city professionals. In 1872, the *New York Times* editorialized about the professional baseball player, calling him "usually a worthless, dissipated gladiator, not much above the professional pugilist in morality and respectability," and likely to throw games at the behest of gamblers. The professional player, said the *Times*, "is an eminently undesirable person and he ought to be peremptorily and completely suppressed. Let our young men meet and play baseball if they choose. They will thus improve their physical well-being without detriment to their morals. To employ professional players to perspire in public for the benefit of gamblers is, however, a benefit to no one. . . ."

Christy's mother worried about the twenty dollars a month he was getting. She understood how a teenager might be distracted from more important things, like studying and preparing for a real profession. She took heart from Christy's resolve to enter college that fall.

She and Gilbert allowed Christy to accept the Honesdale offer, but she later recalled, "I thought it would last a little while and that then my hope of his being a preacher would be realized."

While Christy was enjoying his baseball summer, America was going to war. The U.S.S. *Maine* had been destroyed in Havana harbor in February, and 268 American lives had been lost. Drum-beating news coverage fueled the public's anger, which helped push President William McKinley into retaliating against Spain. In July, as Christy pitched for Honesdale, Theodore Roosevelt was leading his Rough Riders up the hills of Cuban battlefields.

By mid-August, the war was over and America's place in the world had changed. Defeating an atrophied colonial power such as Spain was not the greatest of military feats, but U.S. naval and ground forces had displayed formidable muscle. Americans were proud of their assertion of dominance in the Western hemisphere, and they were quick to embrace warriors such as Roosevelt and Admiral George Dewey.

It was a good time to be a hero, whether in battle or in sport, as Christy was soon to discover.

In September, Christy traveled about a hundred miles west to Lewisburg and entered Bucknell College as a member of the class of 1902. It was the biggest class in the school's history: seventy-five students.

Bucknell was founded by Pennsylvania Baptists in 1846. The campus ranges across wooded hills near the Susquehanna River, and brick storefronts and residences line Market Street. When Christy arrived, Lewisburg was a quiet college town, considerably larger than Factoryville, but still a comfortable home for a boy from a country village.

Christy's course of study at Bucknell was more rigorous than is found at virtually any school today. During his freshman year he took algebra, geometry, trigonometry, French, German, and three Latin courses, reading Livy, Tacitus, and Cicero's *De Senectute*. He did well in all of them; his lowest grade that year was a 90.

He also immersed himself in campus life, joining the band, glee club, literary society, and Phi Gamma Delta fraternity. As class historian, he wrote about the freshman banquet: "On the evening of January 12, they cosily seated themselves in sleighs and drove through the very heart of Lewisburg, giving their class yell in open defiance of the chagrined Sophs. Safely out of town, they leisurely drove to Milton, where a bounteous feast awaited them. Far into the night the banqueters danced, feasted, and listened to the toasters, and when they began their homeward journey they each avowed that they had passed the most delightful evening in their experience."

He was having a wonderful time at Bucknell and soon won national attention for his athletic accomplishments. Although he also played baseball and basketball, he won his collegiate fame on the football field. He was a fullback known for his speed and his ability to evade tacklers at a time when the running game consisted primarily of plunges into the line. In one game he ran sixty-five yards for a touch-down, dancing and sprinting through the entire Susquehanna College team. He was best known, however, for his kicking. As a punter he could boom the ball more than sixty yards. He also mastered the drop-kick, which was particularly valuable because in those days touch-downs and field goals were each worth five points. In one game against Army, Christy drop-kicked a forty-eight-yard field goal from an impos-sible angle, prompting sportswriter Walter Camp to proclaim him "the greatest drop-kicker in intercollegiate competition."

He displayed his work ethic throughout his college athletic career. One of his classmates remembered that in practices, "long after oth-ers had quit around dusk, Matty was still out there practicing drop kicks and punting up and down the field. He would work from differ-ent angles and different distances to be prepared for any sort of emer-gency. He not only played the game but studied it all the time."

Years later, Mathewson remained fond of football. "I'd rather play one good game of football than a dozen games of baseball," he said. He wasn't knocking baseball, it was just that he'd "never drawn the thrill nor the pleasure from it I used to get in a moleskin suit while hitting a line or taking a shot at a field goal in a tight pinch."

But while he was at Bucknell, baseball played a special role for Christy. In addition to pitching for the college team, he continued to make money at the game. The rules governing collegiate amateurs were loose enough to allow Christy to play for pay during the summers.

In 1899, after completing his freshman year, he returned to Honesdale. The town was growing. The local newspaper had just run an article noting that "soon we shall see the horseless carriage on our streets," and debating its merits compared to those of its equine coun-terpart. Local merchants offered "Honest Bicycles at Honest Prices" and bottles of Paine's Celery Compound, which promised to "Make Weak Women Strong."

Christy pitched well, and according to one newspaper account, he "had speed to burn" as he struck out opposing batters. One of his wins was a four-hit victory over the highly regarded Cuban Giants, a black team based in Trenton, New Jersey.

His performance captured the attention of scouts for professional teams, and in mid-July he signed a contract with the Taunton, Massachusetts, team of the New England League. He was to be paid ninety dollars a month, and he believed that "fortune smiled on me." But, he soon decided, fortune "was laughing at me instead." The Taunton team was insolvent, and Christy received only an occasional five dollars from the manager to keep his landlady from evicting him. Finally, the team went under, which turned out to be the best thing that could have happened to the players. They finished the schedule on their own and divided their share of the daily gate receipts.

Christy's record at Taunton was a dismal 2-13. On one occasion, he gave up 19 runs on 24 hits. In his defense, it should be noted that the team was terrible, known for its lengthy losing streaks. In a rare display of frustration, Christy wrote to a Factoryville friend: "I have been accustomed to play on a winning team, but this team makes enough errors of commission and omission to send it to Hades for a protracted period. I pitched in one game where we had ten errors, besides half a dozen passed balls by the catcher. Then again, it is a weak batting team. In two games which I have pitched we have been shut out."

Life with a small-town ball club could, however, be exciting. He wrote: "The New City Hotel in Manchester caught fire at three o'clock in the morning while the Taunton baseball club were stopping there. We had a hot time. It was quite an experience. If you ever get a chance, you want to stop at a hotel that offers such attractions. It is worth your money to find out what people will do when their life's in danger."

By the time he was ready to go back to Pennsylvania, he contemplated walking all the way because he was embarrassed about being so broke. He was able, finally, to put together enough money to get home, and he was happy to return to Bucknell. By now he was disillusioned about baseball and was thinking seriously about a career in forestry, despite his mother's wish that he join the clergy. But for the moment, he devoted his attention to his studies, football, and—most important—women.

Bucknell had begun treating women as serious students in the early 1890s, when its Female Institute became more than a finishing school. Women who completed the institute's program were given sophomore standing at Bucknell and could earn a degree. What seems condescending today was progressive for its time.

The woman who captured most of Christy's attention was Louise Albright, a Bucknell student from the nearby town of Muncy. Years later, one of her friends wrote that Louise "was a very attractive girl, but about the most bashful that I ever recall, and it delighted Christy to see her blush. This was very upsetting to Louise and one reason why she did not accept his proposal to marry her." Instead, Louise introduced Christy to someone better able to deal with his sense of humor, her cousin Jane Stoughton. Jane also attended the Female Institute and was a member of a prosperous Lewisburg family that lived in a big house at 129 Market Street. Jane and Christy hit it off immediately, and the relationship soon became serious. They talked about marriage, but Christy was determined to have financial security before taking that step.

Meanwhile, he continued to perform great feats for Bucknell on the football field. In October 1899, the team traveled to Philadelphia to play the University of Pennsylvania. On the morning of the game, Christy was approached at his hotel by "Phenomenal" Smith, who wanted to talk baseball, not football. Smith was a former big league pitcher who had managed Portland in the New England League and had seen Christy pitching for Taunton.

He told Mathewson, "I'm managing Norfolk next spring, and I'll give you eighty dollars a month to pitch for me." When Christy said, "I had a contract for ninety with Taunton," Smith told him, "But this time you'll get paid; Norfolk is a solid team."

Christy signed a contract on the spot. He then left with his team for the game, where he kicked two field goals, giving Bucknell an unexpected ten points against a Penn team that was a national football power. When he returned to the hotel, Christy ran into Phenomenal Smith again.

"You played a great game this afternoon, and because I liked the way you kicked those two field goals, I'm going to make your salary ninety dollars instead of eighty." He took out the contract and his fountain pen and made the change.

The language of that contract would drive today's players to apoplexy. The ball club had the option of extending the contract for up to three years at the same salary. The club could also "discipline, suspend, fine, or discharge" the player if he was ever "intemperate, immoral, careless, or indifferent," on or off the field, or if he became ill or was injured. The player had no say and no recourse.

Nevertheless, Christy returned to Bucknell pleased with himself. He had done well in the football game and even better in taking care of his financial prospects. The contract with Norfolk gave him solid ground to stand on while dealing with his mother and Jane's family. His mother still hoped he would eventually move from baseball to the church, but she and Gilbert gave him their blessing to go play for Norfolk.

Jane's father was less supportive, telling her, "I can't believe Christy can make a living playing a child's sport with a bunch of uneducated ruffians." After his summer at Taunton, Christy couldn't mount much of an argument to counter Mr. Stoughton's view. So when school was over for the year, he headed to Norfolk to see if he could prove himself.

After what he described as "7 hours and 60 stops" on the train from Lewisburg, he visited Washington for the first time. In a letter to friends at Bucknell, he told of sightseeing at the Capitol, the Navy Yard ("where hundreds of men are making dozzens [sic] of big, mur-derous-looking cannon"), the Smithsonian Museum, and the newly built Library of Congress, which he raved about. He planned to watch the Cornell-Georgetown baseball game the next day, and then take a boat two hundred-some miles down to Norfolk.

He joined the Norfolk team in mid-April, and he was sensational. By early summer he had a record of 20-2, with four shutouts, including a no-hitter. Christy acknowledged that he "was touted as 'Invincible' in the papers around the circuit, and in fact I did have a pretty good record."

He was valuable to the Norfolk club not merely as a winner of games, but also as a marketable commodity. In late June, a Norfolk team official wrote to Andrew Freedman, owner of the New York Giants, telling him that Norfolk "possesses one of the greatest young pitchers that has performed in the Minor Leagues in many a year. It would be worth the trip to look him over. I am assured that he can be secured at a very reasonable figure owing to the financial condition of the league at this writing. He is a man of college education, weight about 165 lbs., big boned, and will take on considerable more weight. He will sure deliver with the proper attention and make a great pitcher. His habits are excellent."

The Giants liked what they heard about Christy, and so did the Philadelphia Athletics. Both offered Norfolk $1,500, and the team let Christy choose where he wanted to go.

"I debated for some time on the question," he later said. "Finally, I chose New York, solely because Philadelphia had a better pitching

staff. I reasoned that as a young, untried pitcher, I would stand a better chance of getting a good workout with the inferior twirling staff
which then represented the New York club."

So the deal with the Giants was made, and Christy Mathewson
was a major leaguer. He was nineteen years old.

TWO

The Strenuous Life

THE NEW YORK GIANTS' newest pitcher made his debut on July 17, 1900, which, at 94 degrees, was the hottest day of the year so far. The next morning's *New York Times* carried a front page list of "deaths and prostrations" caused by the heat.

Whether it was the heat or first-day jitters, something threw Mathewson off stride when he relieved Ed Doheny in the fifth inning of the game against Brooklyn with the score tied 5-5. He promptly gave up two runs—charged to Doheny—and by the end of the game had yielded six more. He allowed three hits, two walks, and he hit three batters. The loss went to Doheny, but Mathewson looked like just another hard-throwing kid who couldn't control where the ball went. The *Times*, however, was charitable in its appraisal: "Mathewson has lots of speed and gives promise of making his way."

The rookie wandered wide-eyed through steamy, clamorous New York. It was so big, so noisy, and there were so many people—the men with high stiff collars and the women with elaborate hats—all in a hurry to get who knows where. Elevated trains rumbled, horses neighed and snorted, street vendors hawked peanuts and gumdrops for five cents a bag. It all swirled around him.

As the summer sun baked the city's inhabitants, baseball was just one of many welcome distractions. Those New Yorkers who had money could let themselves be tempted by ads for resort hotels on

Lake Placid, Long Lake, and elsewhere in the Adirondacks. Closer to home was Coney Island, where it took only a little money to have a wonderful day. You could turn majestically on the Ferris Wheel, race along the Shoot the Chutes ride, or wade genteelly into the Atlantic. If you chose not to leave Manhattan, there was always shopping. Byck Bros. men's outfitters advertised summer suits, regularly $27.50 and $25, on sale for $16.80. Wanamaker's touted its men's hot weather shirts: "One dollar each. You'll not find their match under $1.50."

At the ballpark, Mathewson was roughed up again in his next appearance, surrendering eight runs in seven innings. His performance received little mention in the press, which was devoting its attention to China, where the Boxer Rebellion was underway. The *Times* story on July 26, headlined "China's Millions Prepare for War," reported that "preparations are being made from one end of China to the other for war against the civilized world." The "civilized world" responded with a multinational intervention force that crushed the insurgents and forced China to pay reparations.

As the summer days rolled slowly by, Mathewson felt very much alone and increasingly discouraged. The day after his second outing, he wrote to a Factoryville friend about his prospects of being kept by the Giants.

"At present I have a lame shoulder and don't care a rap about whether they buy me or not. I have finished a couple of games, after the other teams—Pittsburgh and Brooklyn—had knocked out our pitcher. I have not made very brilliant successes in these two games."

There was more to his unhappiness than problems with his pitching. Although he wrote in his letter that "I never have been homesick," he sounded like nothing so much as a teenager who wished he was anywhere but "in my little room here in sweltering New York."

He was living at the Colonial Hotel, a four-story building at the corner of 125th Street and Eighth Avenue. This was the heart of Harlem, which at the time was home primarily to a population of

Irish, Germans, and Jews who had moved uptown from the Lower East Side. It was a vibrant neighborhood. Just up the street from the Colonial was Hurtig and Seamon's Burlesque House, where today the famous Apollo Theater stands. Also on 125th Street was the Harlem Opera House, built in 1889 by Oscar Hammerstein, which a few years later would feature stars such as Fanny Brice and Sophie Tucker. Proctor's vaudeville house was just down the block, as were fashionable stores and restaurants such as Pabst's.

In 1900, New York's population had just passed two million. The *New York Herald* reported the arrival of the first Fifth Avenue autostage—an electric bus with seats for eight people inside and four outside. The fare was five cents. The contract for the city's first subway had just been awarded to John B. McDonald, whose bids for various sections of the line totaled $35 million. A construction boom was underway, and the look of the New York skyline was changing. The buildings climbed higher, and the tallest in the city was now twenty-nine stories, at 13-21 Park Row, downtown.

Young Christy was a long way from small-town Pennsylvania. In a letter to a Factoryville friend he said his parents had written him about the "two- and three-pound pickerel" and "large hauls of eels" being caught in the Tunkhannock; he also mentioned a rumor that "Carrie W."—a Factoryville girl—was "getting prettier every day." He was feeling the tug of home. "Everything in Factoryville seems to be moving in the same serene old way," he wrote. "I would like to spend a few days there." He added that so far only his parents were writing to him, and he reminded his friend of his address: Polo Grounds, New York, NY.

Mathewson became no happier during the remainder of his abbreviated first season. He appeared in six games, all but one in relief, and compiled an 0-3 record with a 5.08 ERA. It was an undistinguished performance for an undistinguished team; the Giants finished in last place, winning 60 games while losing 78.

The Giants were run by Andrew Freedman, who had bought controlling interest for $48,000 in 1895. Between then and 1902, Freedman changed managers sixteen times. He barred unfriendly sportswriters from the ballpark, and had umpire John Heydler fired. (Heydler stayed in baseball and went on to become president of the National League.) Freedman also got into a $200 contract dispute with one of his best players, pitcher Amos Rusie, which caused Rusie to sit out the entire 1896 season.

Major league baseball generally was in the midst of hard times, as most professional teams failed to attract enough fans to be profitable. *Spalding's Official Baseball Guide* reported that "it was not that the patrons of baseball liked the game itself less, but they desired to see fairer and manlier exhibitions on the professional field, and not getting what they wanted, they stayed away."

Mathewson wasn't much help. After one of his games, the *Times* reported that "the New York and St. Louis baseball teams gave about the worst exhibition at the Polo Grounds yesterday that has been seen there in some time." In Mathewson's only start, he did somewhat better, giving up six runs in a complete game that was marked by the Giants' sloppy fielding and weak hitting. A news account reported that "Mathewson pitched a splendid game and deserved to win. A base hit on several occasions would have won the game for New York, but it was not forthcoming."

Mathewson's contract had been purchased from Norfolk on a conditional basis, and at season's end he was returned to the minor league team by the Giants so owner Freedman could recover the $1,500 purchase price. Mathewson was soon drafted by the Cincinnati Reds, who paid Norfolk just $300. Cincinnati then traded him back to the Giants for veteran pitcher Rusie, who was still with the team despite his battles with Freedman. Rusie had once been known as "The Hoosier Thunderbolt," but his arm was so worn out by this time that he lasted through just three games in 1901 before retiring.

Mathewson returned to Bucknell after the 1900 season, but he had lost his enthusiasm for academic life. His grades dropped and he eagerly left school the following April to rejoin the Giants. Junior year was the end of his college education.

Back in New York, he was ready to get to work. After waiting through several days of rain, Mathewson pitched the home opener and got his first big league win, a four-hit 5-3 victory over Brooklyn—the Giants' first win in a home opener in six years. Attendance was 9,800 and, reported the *Times*, "it was the same old baseball crowd—never behind with its advice and always ready to applaud a good play, no matter by whom made." Mathewson, said the paper, "pitched splendid ball."

Giants fans began to envision better days for the team. This Mathewson kid was worth going to the ballpark to watch.

Early in 1901, he was dominant, winning eight straight. A news report about a victory over Philadelphia said that Mathewson had his opponents "completely at his mercy." The description of another Mathewson performance was glowing: "The pitching phenomenon of the New Yorks, Mathewson, again occupied the box and, as usual, his wonderful speed, deceptive change of pace, and sharp curves proved too much for the opposing batsmen." He began by striking out the first batter on three pitches and so excited the crowd that after the game "the bleacherites followed him down to the clubhouse to give him an extra round of cheers." Mathewson's appeal was taking hold.

Some of the games were played in odd circumstances. Mathewson recorded a 2-1 win over Pittsburgh at the Polo Grounds with two players—one from each team—serving as umpires. Giants' owner Freedman had refused to allow umpire Billy Nash into the ballpark, saying that he "did not propose to accept incompetent umpires whose decisions create disorder."

The high point of the year for Mathewson came on July 15 in St. Louis, when he pitched a no-hitter. He ended the season with a 20-

17 record, with 36 complete games in his 38 starts. His ERA was 2.41, and he struck out 221 in 336 innings.

This first 20-win season was a preview of Mathewson's consistency. By the time his career tailed off in 1915, he had won 20 or more games in 13 of his 14 full seasons. But even with his strong perform-ance, in 1901 the Giants were only able to finish seventh, one step out of the cellar.

The young pitcher talked about his success with aw-shucks mod-esty, but he knew how good he was. "As the club was a very inferior one," he later wrote, "this was considered an unusually good record. In all, I made quite a reputation as a young pitcher of promise. The crowds turned out in very encouraging numbers and New York made more money than for several years. The fellows used to come to me after a game and tell me that I ought to be getting a good deal more money. I was receiving $1,500 and had been well content. The salary seemed large to me, but they told me I didn't know anything about it and that such was not the case. They told me that the crowds turned out to see me pitch, and that I ought to shake Freedman down for a good increase."

When Mathewson raised the issue with Freedman in midsea-son, the owner wouldn't agree to a raise, but promised a $500 bonus at season's end. He also bought his pitcher two suits, which, wrote Mathewson, "I needed and was a substantial item from my point of view."

In this era before agents, Mathewson, just twenty-one years old, conducted his own negotiations with Freedman for the following year's salary. On the advice of his teammates, he planned to ask for $5,000.

"This seemed like a stupendous amount of money to me, much too good to be real." When Freedman asked how much he wanted, "I opened my mouth to say $5,000 but the words refused to come. When it came to a showdown, I felt in my soul that no such sum of money existed. So I made a swift mental compromise, and gripping the arms of my chair for support, said in as firm a tone as I could command, $3,500." Freedman, recognizing a bargain, quickly agreed.

Professional baseball had endured a tumultuous time in 1901 due largely to the American League's struggle for parity with the senior National League. Henry Chadwick, editor of the annual *Spalding's Official Baseball Guide*, cited "a spirit of selfish greed" that helped produce "a state of baseball war" between the two leagues. Part of the fight involved a bidding contest that had players jumping from one league to the other, "with what costly consequences," wrote Chadwick, "the depleted club treasuries of the various professional organizations of 1901 plainly show."

Chadwick added, however, that on the amateur level, "the national game flourished to an extent never before equaled in the history of the game. More baseball clubs were organized and more games were played than ever before recorded in a single season." These games, he said, "were witnessed by greater crowds of spectators than ever before gathered." The amateur game was still considered the real baseball, while the professional teams had yet to consistently inspire fans' interest and loyalty.

Mathewson's 20-17 record in 1901 was impressive, but he had gone 11-15 after June 1, and he worried that something was seriously wrong.

"During the winter of 1901 my arm bothered me considerably. The previous summer, I had pitched rather steadily, and like most young twirlers, invariably used all the strength I had regardless of the score or the stage of the game. For a time I got pretty blue, and seriously debated completing my college course, with a view to some other occupation. I was harassed with the idea that my arm would not get into shape, and that I would never be able to pitch as well again."

But he could not bring himself to quit, and based on his performance on opening day 1902, his fears seemed groundless, as he pitched the Giants to a 7-0 win. Thinking that perhaps the Giants would amount to something this year, more than 24,000 fans—the men wearing derbies, the women carrying parasols—were on hand at the Polo Grounds that afternoon. Their enthusiasm was fired by a band playing "There'll Be a Hot Time in the Old Town Tonight," and by the hopefulness that is invariably, if sometimes unrealistically, a part of opening day.

The *Times* reported that "it was a good-natured crowd," although the paper could not resist a condescending reference to the women in attendance. "It was plain that most of the women in the grandstand knew more of golf and ping-pong than they did of the great American game. Their questions to their escorts were a cross between the humorous and pathetic."

When appraising the Giants' pitcher, the *Times* was more respect-ful. "Mathewson was wonderful. He knew exactly when and where to place each ball, and he did it with a skill and judgment which, if kept up, will make him easily the champion pitcher of America."

Mathewson came back four days later to win another game, but his success did not last. He finished 14-17, as the Giants fell back into last place. Despite his mediocre won-lost record, Mathewson's over-all statistics were encouraging. His ERA was 2.11, and he completed 29 of the 32 games he started, including eight shutouts.

That Mathewson was able to perform even that well was surprising given the Giants' chaotic year. After manager Horace Fogel could do no better than an 18-23 start, Freedman replaced him with second base-man Heinie Smith, whose tenure was a disaster, with the team going 5-27. In their desperation, Fogel and Smith tried Mathewson at first base, where his performance was barely average. The Giants were in free-fall, and they threatened to pull Mathewson down with them.

Salvation arrived in the person of twenty-nine-year-old John McGraw, who was hired away from the Baltimore Orioles and took over as manager in July. He brought fiery competitiveness and keen baseball judgment to the forlorn Giants, and would remain with the team for the next thirty years.

He wasted no time in ending the first base experiment.

"The biggest move we made in the latter part of 1902 and 1903," said McGraw, "was rehabilitating Mathewson as a pitcher. The way he developed through encouragement was little short of amazing. With a club of spirit behind him, he burst in bloom overnight, it seemed."

The "club of spirit" was the product of McGraw's acquisition spree, which was made possible by another new arrival, John T. Brush, who bought the team from Freedman. Former majority owner of the Cincinnati ball club, Brush added much-needed stability and business sense to the troubled franchise. Most important, he gave McGraw a free hand in rebuilding the team.

McGraw relied on a straightforward philosophy. "Aggressiveness is the main thing in baseball. The public, I have discovered, doesn't care anything about the methods employed by a ball club. The fan wants to see the home club win. So there is little concern in the mind of the manager as to what the public thinks of his system as long as he wins." As for his own style, "Sportsmanship and easygoing methods are all right, but it is the prospect of a hot fight that brings out the crowds. Personally, I never could see this idea of taking a defeat philosophically. I hate to lose, and I never feel myself beaten until the last man is out. I have tried to instill that same fighting spirit into all the teams I have managed. . . . Namby-pamby methods don't get much in results."

Most of McGraw's players appreciated the manager who was known to the public as the Little Napoleon, but who was always addressed by his players as "Mr. McGraw." They never called him "John" or "Mac" or "Muggsy," which he hated. Outfielder Fred Snodgrass said: "It was an education to play under John J. McGraw. . . . Sometimes Mr. McGraw would bawl the dickens out of me, as he did everybody else. Any *mental* error, any failure to think, and McGraw would be all over you. And I do believe he had the most vicious tongue of any man who ever lived. Absolutely! Sometimes that wasn't very easy to take, you know. However, he'd never get on you for a mechanical mistake, a fielding error or failure to get a hit."

Snodgrass and other Giants noted that McGraw would always stand up for his players. Catcher Chief Meyers said: "According to Mr. McGraw, his ball team never lost a game; he lost it, not his play-ers. He fought for his ballplayers and protected them. You couldn't come around and second-guess McGraw's players without having a fight on your hands right there."

McGraw understood that the personal dynamic between manager and players was all-important. Shortstop Al Bridwell said that McGraw was a great manager "because he knew how to handle men. Some players he rode, and others he didn't. He got the most out of each man. It wasn't so much knowing baseball. All of them know that. . . . What makes the difference is knowing each player and how to handle him. And at that sort of thing, nobody came anywhere close to McGraw."

McGraw and the Giants limped through the remainder of the 1902 season, compiling a 25-38 record. Looking toward next year, McGraw was ready to test his skill at handling players in one specific project: transforming Christy Mathewson from a good pitcher into a superb one.

Writing later about Mathewson at this stage of his career, McGraw said: "As yet he had not begun to study pitching as an art. You must remember that Matty was then but a gangling boy just out of his teens. He simply floundered around in the box with little sense of purpose. By constant efforts at speed he had become wild. . . . He had so many faults that it would be difficult to enumerate them. He simply knew nothing about pitching at all. His wonderful equipment was being wasted."

Fortunately, Mathewson proved to be an eager and intelligent pupil. "I never had to tell Mathewson anything a second time," said McGraw. "From that first day, it seemed, Matty carefully studied all opposing batters. Once he learned what they could hit and what they couldn't, he never forgot. In a few years he had in that wonderful brain of his a chart of nearly every ballplayer in the National League. Realizing that pitching to weaknesses had to be exacting, he started in to perfect his control. He worked and studied all the time."

Whether it was the result of McGraw's teaching, Mathewson's maturing, or a combination of the two, a spectacular improvement in the pitcher's and the team's fortunes was on its way.

Meanwhile the nation was also changing, as a new president brought his personal vigor and ambition to the White House.

He fancied himself an athlete, this wealthy young New Yorker. He had defied his childhood asthma and small stature and vowed to his father, "I'll make my body."

Theodore Roosevelt did his best to fulfill that promise. While a student at Harvard, he boxed, with more tenacity than skill, and was renowned for a "distinctly gory" loss in an intramural championship bout. The blood didn't matter to him, but the defeat rankled.

Roosevelt was ferociously competitive in all his undertakings. As state legislator, cowboy, New York City police commissioner, assistant secretary of the Navy, Rough Rider, and governor of New York, he brought enormous energy and exuberance to whatever task was at hand. By 1900, his political exploits and personal adventures, amplified by skillful self-promotion, had won him a large following throughout the country.

In the midst of gray politicians, he stood out as a colorful celebrity. He wanted action and power, and he wasn't shy about grabbing them both. With popular Republican president William McKinley sure to be renominated in 1900, Roosevelt looked ahead to a presidential campaign of his own in 1904. Some of his support-ers urged him to pursue the vice presidency as his best path to the White House.

A number of his political enemies also thought the vice presidency would be a good place for him. He would be less troublesome there than he had been as an aggressively reformist governor, and if he were to be removed from his home state and his political base, he would be left with little real power. Then, when McKinley finished his second term, the young New Yorker could be shouldered aside and a more conventional Republican selected as the party's nominee. End of Mr. Roosevelt.

But not everyone among Roosevelt's foes was so sure that the vice presidency would be a safe burial ground. Mark Hanna, the Ohio sen-ator who was McKinley's principal political benefactor and one of the most powerful political operatives in the country, worried about Roosevelt's unrestrained zeal for reform and his assertive use of power. "Don't any of you realize," Hanna asked, "that there's only one life between this madman and the White House?"

Nevertheless, Roosevelt was chosen at the GOP convention, and the McKinley-Roosevelt ticket won a landslide victory in November. After being sworn in as vice president in March 1901, Roosevelt found himself with little to do. He presided over the Senate for less than a week, and then Congress adjourned until December. Roosevelt accepted some speaking engagements and planned to spend most of his time on hunting trips and at Sagamore Hill, his home on Long Island.

On September 6, 1901, President McKinley traveled to the Pan American Exposition in Buffalo, New York. As he greeted visitors at the exposition, he was approached by anarchist Leon Czolgosz, who carried a pistol concealed by a handkerchief wrapped around his hand. He shot the president twice at close range.

Roosevelt, who had been attending a luncheon in Vermont,

rushed to Buffalo, where he was assured that McKinley would survive. The vice president then left to join his family for an outing in the Adirondacks. On September 13, as he returned from climbing Mount Tahawus, he was told that the president had taken a turn for the worse and was not expected to live much longer. Roosevelt made another dash to Buffalo by horse-drawn wagon and a special train. While he was en route, McKinley died, humming "Nearer, My God, To Thee" as he slipped out of consciousness.

Roosevelt pledged to "continue unchanged McKinley's policies for the honor and prosperity of the country." But the nation's youngest president soon emerged from his predecessor's shadow. Any presidency is shaped by the incumbent's personality, and in Roosevelt's case that personality was so strong that its influence reached far beyond the White House. Theodore Roosevelt's America would be well suited for the emergence of heroes, on athletic fields and elsewhere.

In 1899, while governor, Roosevelt had delivered a speech in which he urged Americans to vanquish their softness.

"I wish to preach not the doctrine of ignoble ease, but the doctrine of the strenuous life, the life of toil and effort, of labor and strife; to preach that highest form of success which comes, not to the man who desires mere easy peace, but to the man who does not shrink from danger, from hardship, or from bitter toil, and who out of these wins the splendid ultimate triumph."

On another occasion, he praised those who participate over those who merely observe: "The real service is rendered not by the critic who stands aloof from the contest, but by the man who enters into it and bears his part as a man should, undeterred by the blood and the sweat." He added, "It is of far more importance that a man shall play something himself, even if he plays it badly, than that he shall go with hundreds of companions to see someone else play well."

He extolled individual and collective toughness, and stressed the importance of personal and national resolve. He criticized the "mol-lycoddle vote—the people who are soft physically and morally," who he said were a factor in the United States being unprepared to fight the wars, such as the one against Spain in 1898, that an aspiring world power might find necessary.

Roosevelt returned to these themes time and again in his speeches and writings. As president, he wanted to foster prosperity and peace, but he could not tolerate the self-satisfaction and laziness they could spawn. He saw himself as the nation's energizer and guardian against sloth.

Americans were confident of their standing in the world following the Spanish-American War in which Roosevelt and his Rough Riders had gained much fame. Now the country had to decide what to do next. Still viewed as an adolescent—although an increasingly muscular one—by world powers, the United States was on the threshold of the international leadership role it would assume in its next war, which was not too many years in the future. Roosevelt seemed to sense the impor-tance of seizing the time and building national character.

The nation shared Roosevelt's ambitious confidence. There were 76 million Americans in 1900, and their vision extended far beyond their own country's borders. Among politicians, debate persisted about the wisdom of "expansionism," as its advocates called it, or "imperialism," as it was termed by critics.

At home, big changes were taking hold. Automobiles, and con-crete roads for them to ride on, were becoming more common. The number of cars on U.S. roads grew rapidly, from 300 in 1895 to about 78,000 by 1905. Some predicted, however, that the automobile would never become as commonly used as the bicycle. Newspapers announced that "the day is coming when practically every household will have a telephone." The six-day, sixty-hour work week was shrink-ing, giving workers time to enjoy diversions at ballparks and else-where.

As America developed its muscle and extended its reach, the president was an intense missionary and energetic cheerleader. Pictures of Roosevelt campaigning show him leaning out over the crowd from a speaker's platform or the back of a railroad car, shaking his fist as he made his point. It is tempting to suggest that he thundered in his speeches; his look is that of one who roars. But recordings of Roosevelt reveal an aristocrat's lilt rather than a warrior's growl.

Nevertheless, he delivered his message forcefully. He considered athletics to be one way to strengthen American resolve. Sports were useful, he said, "because they encourage a true democratic spirit; for in the athletic field the man must be judged not with reference to outside and accidental attributes, but to that combination of bodily vigor and moral quality which go to make up prowess." He himself had been knocked to the canvas in the boxing ring and bucked off horses in the Dakota Territory. This was the kind of participatory "strife" that he believed would build character in his countrymen.

Roosevelt's combativeness was partly a response to the jeering that had greeted his entry into politics during the 1880s. Newspapers had noted his mannered speaking style and appearance and pronounced him a "dude," a "weakling," and a "Jane Dandy." One even referred to him as "Oscar Wilde." Roosevelt was enraged at being compared to a foppish dilettante, and he knew his political future would be in jeopardy unless he could change his image. He responded to aspersions about his masculinity by recasting himself as the cowboy-tough Rough Rider and an advocate of the rigorous testing that occurred on the playing field.

Roosevelt preferred amateur over professional sports, but he singled out professional baseball as the sport that best maintained its ties to its amateur roots. "In baseball alone," he wrote, "the professional teams . . . have preserved a fairly close connection with non-professional players, and have done good work in popularizing a more admirable and characteristic American game." But, he cautioned, "professionalism is the curse of many an athletic sport, and the chief obstacle to its healthy development."

He placed higher value on academic achievement and civic involvement, chastising those amateur sportsmen who did nothing further with their lives and tried to perpetuate their athletic glory. "With very few exceptions," he wrote, "the man who makes some athletic pursuit his main business, instead of turning to it as a health-giving pastime, ceases to be a particularly useful citizen." He added that "the amateur athlete who thinks of nothing but athletics, and makes it the serious business of his life, becomes a bore, if nothing worse. A young man who has broken a running or jumping record, who has stroked his winning club crew, or played on his college nine or eleven, has a distinct claim to our respect; but if, when middle-aged, he has still done nothing more in the world, he forfeits even this claim which he originally had."

Roosevelt's disdain for the college athlete who rested on his laurels was seconded by Joseph Raycroft, a Princeton administrator and president of the Intercollegiate Basketball Association, who criticized the idea of amateur athletes moving into professional sports. "It seems to me," said Raycroft, "that a college graduate should fulfill a greater position in life than that which is open to him as a professional athlete. However, I do not hold that there is anything dishonorable about professional athletics, but this field does not afford the college man a broad enough scope for the full use of the advantages which his college training has given him."

This was the prevailing opinion at the beginning of the century, and was the backdrop for Mathewson's arrival on the professional sports scene. The amateur was cheered while the professional was viewed with skepticism.

Mathewson did much to change this. He was the first highly visible sports star to prove that a college education and a professional athletic career were not necessarily incompatible. He personified the growing belief that college athletes who became pros need not sacrifice their integrity when they played for money; rather, they could use the intellectual and social skills acquired in college to elevate their sports.

It helped that he wasn't alone; Mathewson was part of the first wave of college-educated ballplayers. Between 1901 and 1910, about 22 percent of major league rookies were collegians. The following decade, the figure rose to 28 percent.

In the public's mind, the principal distinction between collegians and other ballplayers was not education per se, but rather the differences in their personal styles and manners. When Mathewson arrived in the majors, most first class and many second class hotels would not host big league teams for fear that the players' behavior would offend other guests. The hotels that did admit ballplayers often made them eat in a separate dining room. Players were well known for pinching waitresses and wrecking furniture, and if they didn't like the steaks they were served, they would nail them to the restaurant's walls.

In this world, Mathewson stood out. He was soft spoken and well spoken. He was a fierce competitor on the diamond, but he left his ferocity at the ballpark. He had been shaped by his parents' teaching and by the standards at Keystone and Bucknell. He later wrote, "I had been brought up rather strictly among sober country folks who considered the evils of drink a national calamity and criticized many things to which New York would never give a second thought."

This was a different upbringing than most ballplayers had known. Many had come from far lower on the economic ladder, escaping factory or farm to play ball, and for them big league life was one long roughhouse. Some of the public thought this was fine, but many baseball fans were put off by it. They preferred the amateur game, and would turn out to watch Princeton or Yale play, but wanted no association with the rowdy breed of pro ballplayers.

Mathewson was different. He was someone fans could identify with—a professional, but still a player they and their children could admire and emulate. They would buy tickets to watch him play.

In nonpolitical ways, Mathewson was an exemplar of American character in the Roosevelt era. For one thing, he showed that it was possible to strike a balance between athletics and the rest of one's life, maintaining personal values. That approach met Roosevelt's approval. In a letter to his son Ted, Roosevelt wrote, "Athletic proficiency is a mighty good servant, and like so many other good servants, a mighty bad master."

Throughout Roosevelt's writings, references to character are often couched in terms related to athletics. "There is need," he said, "of a sound body, and even more need of a sound mind. But above mind and above body stands character—the sum of those qualities which we mean when we speak of a man's force and courage, of his good faith and sense of honor."

Echoing Roosevelt was editor and social critic Herbert Croly, whose influential 1909 book, *The Promise of American Life*, endorsed an assertive nationalism. Croly wrote that "men endowed with high moral gifts and capable of exceptional moral achievements have also their special part to play in the building of an enduring democratic structure." Croly noted the importance of role models. "The common citizen," he wrote, "can become something of a saint and something of a hero, not by growing to heroic proportions in his own person, but by the sincere and enthusiastic imitation of heroes and saints, and whether or not he will ever come to such imitation will depend upon the ability of his exceptional fellow countrymen to offer him acceptable examples of heroism and saintliness."

Who would meet the standards Roosevelt and Croly were prescribing? The president did not identify any individual as the paragon he envisioned, but an athlete could certainly possess appeal that transcended partisanship and social class. As Christy Mathewson's career progressed and his fame grew, he would fit comfortably into this Rooseveltian mold.

Roosevelt was presiding over a very different White House. With a brood of young children, plus their cousins and friends, the Roosevelts found that the executive mansion sometimes resembled a sports stadium. The hallways, the children decided, were fine places for races on foot and on roller skates. Son Quentin brought his school baseball team to play on the White House grounds, where he had marked out a diamond.

The president himself was not much of a baseball fan because his eyesight wasn't good enough for him to see what was going on in the far reaches of a ballpark. But he wrote, "I like to see Quentin practicing baseball. It gives me hope that one of my boys will not take after his father in this respect, and will prove able to play the national game."

Not in the least inhibited by the stately character of his home and job, Roosevelt reveled in having athleticism all around him. One of his friends wrote, "You must always remember that the President is about six." Roosevelt proudly told his son Kermit, "I am wrestling with two Japanese wrestlers three times a week. I am not the age or the build one would think to be whirled lightly over an opponent's head and batted down on a mattress without damage. But they are so skillful that I have not been hurt at all." The following month, however, he cataloged for his son Ted all the bruises and swelling his wrestling had produced. Despite being battered, he delighted in the sport, noting that the wrestlers "have taught me three new throws that are perfect corkers."

Roosevelt carefully considered the social compact and the relationship between government and citizen. The individual responsibility he had defined as part of "the strenuous life" would remain essential, but it would be part of a larger concept of community. "When all is said and done," he told Congress, "the rule of brotherhood remains as the indispensable prerequisite to success in the kind of national life for which we strive. Each man must work for himself, and unless he so works no outside help can avail him. But each man must remember also that he is indeed his brother's keeper, and that while no man who refuses to walk can be carried with advantage to himself or anyone else, yet that each at times stumbles or halts, that each at times needs to have the helping hand outstretched to him."

This endorsement of generosity and teamwork was very much in line with Roosevelt's pronouncements about the importance of "character." It helped focus public attention on the nobility of purpose that a Rooseveltian hero—in politics, athletics, or any other field—would exemplify. This political outlook dovetailed with elevated standards of sportsmanship. On the athletic field, the noble citizen as defined by Roosevelt would not only excel at his sport, but would treat teammates and opponents graciously and refrain from disputes with umpires or other officials. This athletic noblesse oblige would become the hallmark of Mathewson's on-field behavior.

The working classes whose concerns Roosevelt addressed were increasingly embracing baseball. Between 1903 and 1908, major league attendance doubled, which led team owners to expand their ballparks or build new ones. The Giants had the highest attendance in 1908—910,000—and reached nearly five million for the decade. Baseball historian Bill James writes that the main causes of this surge were "the effective control of vulgarity and unseemly behavior on the field, a series of outstanding pennant races, and a huge popular interest in the World Series," which became particularly intense beginning in 1905.

Historian Steven Riess identifies a number of factors beyond baseball itself that spurred the expansion: cities' rapid growth, which meant a larger fan base; a higher standard of living—especially for the middle class—which meant more disposable income and leisure time; and mass transit, such as electric streetcars, which enabled fans to get to games easily and inexpensively.

Riess notes that there has long been debate about who the fans were at this time. He says the people going to most of the games were middle-class workers with the job schedule and money to attend. According to catcher Chief Meyers, the Giants didn't start their weekday games until four o'clock because "the stock market didn't close until three o'clock, and then two or three thousand people who worked down at Wall Street would take the elevated train up to the Polo Grounds." The lower-class fans followed their favorite teams and players through the penny press, and attended games when they could.

A variety of factors enhanced baseball's appeal: the rivalry between (and sometimes within) teams' cities; the attention given by the press to the game's heroes; and the simple pleasures of joining thousands of others on a sunny day at the ballpark. Expanding the fan base was always important to baseball's leadership. Efforts were made to get more women to attend games, enticing them initially with free admission on "Ladies' Days." The owners did this knowing that some efforts to recruit female fans had produced unanticipated results. In 1897, the Washington Senators had tried to take advantage of pitcher Win Mercer's popularity among women by admitting all women free to one of his games. But when Mercer was ejected from the game, the women attacked the umpire, ripped out seats, and broke windows. That was the end, for a while, of "Ladies' Days" in Washington. In later years, teams tried other methods to attract women fans, such as encouraging suffragists to buy discounted blocs of tickets and then resell them to raise funds for their cause.

At the heart of baseball's fan support were those of all ages who played the game themselves. In this regard, the sport had no shortage of proselytizers. As the 1903 season was beginning, William Randolph Hearst wrote that "every father of a normal boy should insist that his boy should play baseball as often and as much as he can. This is not only for the good of his body, but for the good of his mind and his morals. . . . Baseball is most excellent training for character. It imperatively demands and develops and forces a swift and accurate judgment and the habit of quick thinking. . . . Every American boy ought to play baseball, and be proud of it as a great national institution."

Other national institutions were changing, while some resisted change. President Roosevelt shocked many by having lunch with Booker T. Washington at the White House in October 1901. Nevertheless, lynching continued with frightening regularity, and the U.S. Supreme Court in 1903 upheld state measures blocking African-American voting. On racial issues, Roosevelt moved with uncharacteristic caution, understanding the political repercussions that would follow any attempts to impose true reform.

He was more successful on other fronts, skillfully challenging the arrogance of great wealth, personified by the likes of J. P. Morgan, who once said, "I owe the public nothing." As Roosevelt demonized those who displayed that kind of selfishness, he sought to establish an alternative paragon—be it a courageous politician or a noble athlete.

Modernization was accelerating and society was becoming more impersonal. Baseball, however, remained an anchor that could keep the idea of community from drifting away. As a sport to be played and to be watched, its constituency remained faithful even as the game changed. Just as the presidency was being altered as a function of Roosevelt's assertive leadership, so too was baseball evolving because of the growing focus on individual players.

Christy Mathewson was increasingly prominent among them. Grantland Rice later wrote that Mathewson "brought something to baseball that no one else had ever given the game. He handed the game a certain touch of class, an indefinable lift in culture, brains, and personality." As 1903 began, Mathewson had a remarkable year awaiting him—he would now establish himself as baseball's first superstar.

Before that, however, he had other matters to attend to. On March 5, 1903, he married Jane Stoughton at her parents' home in Lewisburg. The announcement caught some by surprise. One of the New York papers reported that while he was at Bucknell "his calls upon Miss Stoughton were not frequent enough to cause any comment, and it was not until he left college to play baseball that the busybodies of the small town regarded his intentions as serious." Another newspaper reported that after the engagement had been announced, the former Baptist Mathewson "was received into the membership of the First Presbyterian Church, presumably through the influence of his fiancee."

The Lewisburg newspaper touted the wedding as "one of the most fashionable of the season," and noted that "Mrs. Mathewson is a young lady of charming disposition, and has many accomplishments and a host of friends."

After the wedding, when the couple boarded the Buffalo Flyer to leave for their honeymoon, they found that Mathewson's college fraternity brothers had distributed handbills proclaiming: "Christy Mathewson, New York's great baseball pitcher, and newly wedded wife are on this train. Make them feel at home, as there may be Something Doing. Note: He will be easily recognized by his boyish countenance and Apollo-like form."

With this send-off, the Mathewsons were on their way. The train sped south toward their honeymoon destination: Savannah, Georgia, spring training site of the New York Giants.

THREE

Marvelous Matty

THE TWO WOMEN KEPT THEIR DISTANCE but watched each other carefully.

"We sat in the lobby of the De Soto Hotel for hours, days it seemed, each staring when the other wasn't looking. She had gray eyes and dark brown hair. She was dressed rather nicely, I thought. This was not a catty reaction. It seemed fitting and quite in character because she came from a somewhat strait-laced family. . . .

"And she was a Sunday-school teacher, which also made her suspect. I caught her staring at me a few times, thinking narrow thoughts, perhaps, if I was any judge of appearance. . . .

"I wore a new dress that was generously sprinkled with sequins, and the very latest thing in New York. Also, on my left hand was the dazzling engagement ring that reflected my husband's pride and affection. It represented something else to the bride across the lobby. She actually thought, 'Only a hussy would wear a ring like that!' "

That was Mrs. John McGraw's initial appraisal of the "bride across the lobby," Mrs. Christy Mathewson. But soon Blanche McGraw and Jane Mathewson stopped staring and started talking, and before long they were shopping together and laughing about their early wariness of one another.

The friendship between the couples grew stronger, and when the 1903 season began they decided to share an apartment at Eighty-fifth

Street and Columbus Avenue. A block from Central Park, the fur-nished seven-room residence rented for fifty dollars a month.

This was a relatively new and growing neighborhood. The Ninth Avenue elevated line, which had begun service in 1879, spurred development of town houses and apartment buildings in the area. One resident recalled that at the turn of the century "the streets were mostly empty and quiet. The loudest noises were the sounds of the horses' feet clip-clopping on the cobblestones as the hansom cabs and open carriages drove down the street. I would hear that along with the rumbling of the El and the newsboys shouting 'Extra!' when I was lying in bed at night."

In this haven, the two men talked baseball constantly, replaying past contests and debating strategies they might use in the future. McGraw said, "Together we made a study of the batting weaknesses of the opposing players in the league." At ten o'clock each morning during a home stand, they left together for the Polo Grounds and the education of the young pitcher continued. McGraw wrote that his pupil "had an unusual store of common sense and, being well educated, was eager to be directed. Mathewson never forgot anything in his life."

Mathewson was only one of McGraw's projects. The manager was determined to change the character of the Giants by infusing the team with his own combative spirit. He got results quickly. In 1903, the Giants moved from last place to second, from a 48-88 record to 84-55. Mathewson was a big reason for the change, going 30-13 in the first of his four seasons of 30 or more wins. McGraw also received a stellar performance from Joe McGinnity, who put together a 31-20 record. The Giants were now a team to be taken seriously by the rest of the National League.

The friendship between Mathewson and McGraw was one of tem-peramental opposites. Mathewson went about his business quietly; McGraw had a flair for drama when it might fire up his team. During a game against Cincinnati, when McGraw thought the Giants were getting too many bad calls from umpire Bill Byron, he stormed onto the field, grabbed Byron's pocket watch, and stomped on it. That got the manager ejected, but it roused his players. The next day, McGraw bought Byron a better watch than the one he smashed.

On another occasion, when Barney Dreyfuss, the president of the Pittsburgh club, was sitting in a box seat at a Giants-Pirates game, McGraw screamed at him, accusing him of being crooked and controlling the league's umpires. Such stunts earned McGraw ejections and fines, but the newly fiery Giants kept winning. Team owner John Brush defended his manager, telling reporters that McGraw "is not given credit for frequent self-suppression." That did not appease everyone. One writer believed "the obstreperous Muggsy had reached the limit of rowdyism and I kept hoping that after each offense against decency it would be his last. All to no purpose, for he appears to be irrepressible and he is beyond redemption." Another reporter accused McGraw and the Giants of "hoodlum tactics and general disorder on the ball field."

Mathewson rarely jumped into a McGraw-instigated fracas. He understood that everything the manager did had a purpose, whether it was to unsettle the opposing team, inspire his own players, or in some other way give the Giants just a bit of an edge. As the Giants improved, Mathewson recognized McGraw's effectiveness. "On the field he is the captain-general and everybody knows it. Off the field he is a member of the team and the personal friend of every man. Therein lies the difference between other managers and McGraw."

Mathewson also noted that "the brain of McGraw is behind each game the Giants play, and he plans every move, most of the hitters going to the plate with definite instructions from him as to what to try to do. In order to make this system efficient, absolute discipline must be assured. If a player has other ideas than McGraw as to what should be done, Mac's invariable answer to him is, 'You do what I tell you, and I'll take the responsibility if we lose.'"

McGraw reciprocated this respect. "Mathewson's sole object was to win the ball game for you, and he seldom showed opposing hitters all his stuff until they had men on the bases in position to score. He holds all records for leaving men on base." Even on bad days, said McGraw, "I rarely took Matty out. I always felt that somehow he was better than anyone who would take his place." Jane Mathewson said McGraw never removed her husband from a game, but when the situation called for it, Christy would take himself out.

McGraw liked smart ballplayers, and looked for players who had been to college or had at least finished high school. "I seek boys who can think, who have initiative, who can reason things out, who have enough brains to be loyal and ambitious, and who have enough balance and pride to be dependable." Based on those criteria, Mathewson was his ideal player. "In a critical situation, watching Matty was just as comfortable as sitting behind four aces in a poker game. . . . Always he worked for the club and with the club, whether in the game or not. When he became a master of his trade he was an inspiration to other pitchers."

Mathewson's take-charge attitude reportedly led to one of the rare conflicts between the two men. The first game of the 1905 World Series between the Giants and the Philadelphia Athletics was scoreless after four innings, and a nervous McGraw told his outfielders to look to him for signals about where to position themselves. This breached McGraw's agreement that Mathewson—alone among the Giants' pitchers—would tell his fielders where to play based on how he planned to pitch the batter. When Harry Davis, who had led the American League in home runs that year (with eight), came to the plate, Mathewson turned his back to home plate and waved his outfielders into position. When he turned back to face the batter, McGraw signaled the outfielders to move. Mathewson saw this, once again turned his back to the plate, and again indicated to his outfielders where he wanted them to be. Knowing better than to anger McGraw, the outfielders ignored Mathewson.

After glancing at McGraw, Mathewson made no further attempt to move the outfielders. He focused on the batters and struck out all three Athletics he faced that inning. His unspoken message to McGraw: If you don't let me run the game on the field, I won't let anyone hit the ball, even if it means I won't last nine innings. McGraw understood and let Mathewson resume his role as on-field commander.

This is one of those stories that exists on the fringes of baseball lore but is impossible to verify. It was told by Jimmy McAleer, a player, manager, and baseball executive who in 1905 was managing the St. Louis Browns. Although the details of his account don't quite fit with the facts of the game, the story rings true: an aggressive and nervous John McGraw, managing the underdogs, wanting to control every aspect of his team's performance in the championship series; a cool but fiercely competitive Mathewson, confident in his skill. Given the two men's strong wills, a collision like this almost certainly happened, and not just once.

The 1905 World Series may have been Mathewson's finest perform-ance. The Giants were thought to be no match for Connie Mack's Philadelphia Athletics, who were led by pitchers Eddie Plank and Chief Bender. But in the first game Mathewson shut down the Athletics on four hits, and the Giants won 3-0. The *New York Times* praised "McGraw's magnificent baseball machine, its every cog and wheel oiled and smoothed to a nicety," and singled out "Manhattan's masterly Matty, who by his brain and brawn, cleverness and strength, more than did his share to bring the first victory of the series to New York. . . . Mathewson did everything that was desired. His speed was terrific, his control perfect. He alternated slow and fast ones. He used the wet ball [then legal]. He curved them in, out, down, and over. Philadelphia was at his mercy."

The *Times* also reported that McGraw had bet $400 on his team. There were no objections. The wager was seen as evidence of wis-dom, not misbehavior.

After the Athletics won the second game, also 3-0, behind Bender's four-hitter, Mathewson returned on two days' rest. He pitched yet another four-hitter, winning this time 9-0, and was praised by the *Times* as the "professor of occult speed and pretzel curve." Mathewson's teammate Joe McGinnity won game four, and Mathewson wrapped up the series with his third shutout. "And be it recorded right here," said the *Times*, "that New York possesses the pitching marvel of the century." Mathewson, said the paper, "bestrode the field like a mighty Colossus."

Twenty-seven innings pitched, no runs, fourteen hits, one walk, eighteen strikeouts—all this within the span of six days. It was one of the greatest baseball feats of all time.

Fans throughout the country read about and talked about his performance. Boys on sandlots imagined themselves as Christy Mathewson. Casual followers of baseball became more interested, checking the newspapers for reports about the young Giants pitcher. Stories about his pitching skills and gentlemanly character were told and retold. Mathewson had become a superstar.

Only a few moments of film of Mathewson pitching remain today. The best footage—three pitches worth—is found in a 1907 short titled "Christy Mathewson and the New York National League Team." He displays a classic overhand delivery, with a moderately high leg kick. Nothing tricky. Everything in his motion is smooth and graceful.

As McGraw and others noted, Mathewson combined physical skill with intelligence. He knew that the pitcher had the advantage. "It is mathematically poor dope for the batter to outguess the pitcher," Mathewson said. "The odds are heavily against him. There are too many things the pitcher can do if he chooses." Mathewson later wrote: "It takes a pitcher a long while to learn the tricks and eccentricities of the batsmen. No two batters should be treated alike. A pitcher should be a pretty close student of human nature. Each rival batter should be studied, analyzed and catalogued in a cerebral pigeon-hole." This mental filing system eventually helped him extend his career. Jane wrote that "after he had used up his early supply of youthful vigor, he remained a great pitcher for years by pitching with his mind. His brain had card-indexed all the pitches he had thrown to various batters and his mathematical mind had figured out the percentage of a batter hitting every kind of pitch he had at his command."

Beyond his smart approach to the game, Mathewson's greatest asset was his responsiveness to adversity—"pitching in a pinch," he called it. In an account of an eleven-hit shutout he pitched in 1907, the *Times* wrote: "While Matty was pounded hard enough to lose under ordinary circumstances, he had the good fortune to keep the smashes scattered. In tight situations, a number of which materialized during the afternoon, he was at his best, and the way he toyed with his rivals at these times was a sight to behold. . . . Matty would put an extra twist in his arm, and either make his opponents fan or perish on easily fielded balls." On another occasion—a no-hitter that Mathewson pitched in 1905—a reporter wrote that the opposing players were "made to look like animated automata of putty."

But even media darlings are eventually scorched by journalists. Mathewson went through a four-game losing streak in May 1908, and after the third of these losses, a newspaper cited his "miserable exhibition" and said that "judged by his performance in the last three games in which he has pitched, the star of Christy Mathewson has set." When he lost the fourth in the string, the *Times* wrote that "the erstwhile 'great Matty' was driven from the rubber. All signs of his former greatness had flown by the time the Cubs got through with him."

The vultures had gathered prematurely. Mathewson quickly returned to his usual form and ended the 1908 season with a record of 37-11. That remains the most wins in a single season by a National League pitcher.

Near the end of the 1908 season, Mathewson encountered one of the incidents of bad luck that plagued him and the Giants as they pursued another world championship. On September 23, in a crucial game in New York against the Chicago Cubs, Mathewson and Chicago's Jack Pfiester were pitching superbly, and the game was tied 1-1 going into the bottom of the ninth. With two out, the Giants' Harry McCormick was on third and nineteen-year-old rookie Fred Merkle was on first. Al Bridwell lined a hit into right center and McCormick trotted home with the winning run. As was common practice, Merkle didn't bother to run all the way to second after seeing McCormick score and instead headed for the clubhouse. Thousands of fans poured onto the field.

Chicago second baseman Johnny Evers yelled for center fielder Solly Hofman to throw him the ball. Evers knew that if he touched second, it would be a force-out of the now departed Merkle—the third out of the inning—and McCormick's run wouldn't count. Giants pitcher Joe McGinnity, heading for the clubhouse, saw Evers calling for the ball and realized that nothing good could come of his getting it. So he intercepted Hofman's throw and hurled the ball toward the left field bleachers. Somehow, Evers retrieved the ball—or at least *a* ball—and stepped on second. He looked around for an umpire, but neither of the two working the game had seen the play.

The Cubs appealed, and that night home plate umpire Hank O'Day ruled that Merkle was out and the game was a tie. He said he hadn't resumed play because it was too dark.

As it turned out, this Chicago victory meant that the season ended with the Cubs and the Giants tied for first, necessitating a play-off. The Giants and their fans believed they had won the September 23 game and the pennant. The New York players almost refused to play, taking the field only after team owner John Brush, lying ill in his bed at the Lambs Club, urged them to do so. On the afternoon of the play-off game, wrote Mathewson, "the nerves of the players were rasped raw with the strain, and the town wore a fringe of nervous prostration."

Again it was Mathewson versus Pfiester, who was ineffective and was quickly replaced by Mordecai Brown, who was at the top of his game. The Cubs won, 4-2.

Mathewson said of his own performance: "My part in the game was small. I started to pitch and I didn't finish. The Cubs beat me because I never had less on the ball in my life." And so the Cubs went to the World Series instead of the Giants.

Years later, another facet of Mathewson's involvement in this episode became known. Before the position of baseball commissioner was created, a board of directors governed the league. These directors had to decide if the tiebreaker should be played, or if the Giants should be awarded the pennant. The determinative issue was whether Merkle had made it to second base.

One of the directors, George Dovey, recalled that there were "affidavits from both sides galore" claiming that the other side was lying about what had happened at the game. Then they came across Mathewson's affidavit. He had been coaching at first base and said that Merkle had not, in fact, gone all the way to second.

Dovey said: "You may not realize what that affidavit, offered to us voluntarily, meant to Mathewson. First of all, it meant a share in the World Series. Also, had the disputed game stood as it ended, without technicality, Mathewson would have led all National League pitchers for the season. Miner [Mordecai] Brown beat him out of the honor in the post-season game. We took all the other affidavits and threw them in the waste basket. Matty's word was good enough for us."

During the first decade of his major league career, Mathewson won 263 games while losing 121. By virtue of being on one of baseball's best teams and being located in the nation's largest city, his fame continued to grow rapidly. Responding to fans' interest, sportswriters scrutinized his technique. Mathewson himself discussed his craft in interviews and in articles he wrote. "A pitcher needs very little power, provided he has control and uses his strength intelligently. . . . I would rather have a pitcher who has only moderate speed and a fair curve, but knows how to use them. . . . To me control is the first require-ment of good pitching."

He had carefully considered how a pitcher could best use his body. "In the first place, it takes a good physical specimen of manhood to make a successful twirler. Knotted muscles, however, are not an essential to a great pitcher, as the ball is propelled mainly by a swing of the body, and the bulk of the power is derived from the back and shoulders, the arm acting as a whipcord to snap the ball. In fact, the more a pitcher can learn to get the power from his body the more he will save his arm. . . . I attribute a great deal of my success to my abil-ity to get most of the propelling force from the swing of the body."

As to his own strengths, Mathewson said: "I have always thought my curve was my best pitch. At least it has been my favorite. . . . When mastered, there is no more successful ball than the drop or drop curve. It is a ball that can be made to break very abruptly or a gradual break can be put to it. When it breaks quickly, the batter invariably hits over it and misses it entirely. It is the ball I usually rely upon when there is a man on third base and no one out."

Besides the curve and its conventional variations, he had devel-oped a rare weapon during his days pitching for Honesdale: the fade-away. Coupled with his standard pitches, this made Mathewson all the more devastating. He wrote: "I use it in every game and it has never failed me in recent years when my control was in working order. It is the ball that has won for me all my honors in baseball."

Mathewson defined it as "a ball that curves out from a left-handed batter" when thrown by a right-handed pitcher. Today it is known as a screwball, made famous by a later Giants pitcher, Carl Hubbell. To throw it Mathewson changed his delivery from straight overhand to a slight angle, noting that "this motion is gone through so quickly, however, that it is practically impossible for the batsman to detect the fact that he is going to get something very different from a drop curve." At release, he twisted his hand sharply inward, to the left, "and the loosely held ball, which is revolving from the rapid action of the arm, slips out sideways, or off the second finger. . . . When the ball leaves the hand, the arm is so twisted that the palm of the hand faces outward."

Although throwing the pitch sounds painful (and many coaches would argue that such a twisting motion can wreck a pitcher's arm), Mathewson made it work for years. He later noted, "I have tried to teach several big league pitchers how to throw the fade-away and not one of them has succeeded. The difficulty is that too much attention is required. The fade-away is a difficult ball to control."

His formidable array of pitches was further enhanced by his poise. The raw competitiveness of baseball at the time, exemplified by McGraw's willingness to bait players, umpires, fans and anyone else, made a player's temperament especially important. On a team such as the Giants, almost always in the running for a championship and therefore a favorite target for rival teams, stress was intense and constant. Mathewson flourished in that environment. He wrote: "It is in the pinch that the pitcher shows whether or not he is a big leaguer. He must have something besides curves then. He needs a head, and he has to use it. It is the acid test. That is the reason so many men, who shine in the minor leagues, fail to make good in the majors. They cannot stand the fire."

For New York, the Giants' rise was just one example of change in the city's life. In 1902, immigration into the United States—mostly coming through New York—was expanding steadily. In January of that year, 18,000 newcomers arrived; in February, 30,000; in March, 57,000; in April, 74,000. Most of these new residents came from

Italy, Austria-Hungary, and Russia. During the century's first decade, nine million legal immigrants arrived, and by 1910 roughly 15 percent of Americans were foreign-born.

The look of the city was also evolving—it was getting taller and more crowded. In July 1907, for example, a newspaper reported plans for a twelve-story office building to be constructed at the corner of Park Avenue and Forty-first Street, "anticipating increased demand for offices near Grand Central Station."

As their city grew, New Yorkers examined themselves in literary mirrors. On October 15, 1905, in the same edition that reported the Giants' championship, the *Times* reviewed several books that were critical of New York life. One of these was Edith Wharton's new novel, *The House of Mirth*. Praised as "a paragon of artistic excellence" and "a novel of remarkable power," the book, said the *Times*, "will have great vogue because the sins and shortcomings of New York's fashionable life are set forth in it by one who can speak of them with a sophisticated utterance from first-hand knowledge."

The House of Mirth enjoyed the most rapid sales of any book ever published by Scribner's—140,000 copies within three months. When told that she had "stripped" New York society, Wharton demurred, saying that "New York society is still amply clad," and that she had shown "only that little atrophied organ—the group of idle and dull people—that exists in any big and wealthy social body." Nevertheless, Wharton also noted the "flatness and futility" of fashionable New York, exemplified in the novel by the demise of Lily Bart in the midst of cruelly frivolous and indifferent high society.

Mathewson never joined the debased and debasing social circles that Wharton portrayed. Despite his access to New York's high life, he remained wary. After the 1905 World Series, the *New York Herald* observed that "New York City is the one place in the country where they kill a successful man by kindness, and it doesn't matter whether he is a minister or a prize fighter. Men with money, in the overweening desire to be seen with a notable in any walk of life, will lavish every form of hospitality, and when this is repeated night after night, the muscles begin to sag, the fat grows about the lungs, and the eyes are dimmed. Mathewson said 'no' to the very first invitation. . . . He has maintained this same attitude ever since. Probably he is known personally to fewer baseball enthusiasts in New York City than any other star that ever appeared regularly for the home team."

He was successful and acclaimed, and although he tried to keep a low profile, he was an object of curiosity. His privacy was periodically invaded by fans and journalists, but the results were usually benign. Fans sometimes called the Mathewsons' apartment to ask when Christy would be pitching. The press was also persistent. Jane Mathewson became skillful at crafting shrewd responses to reporters' questions. Asked by one if she was a suffragette, she said, "No, I'm not, though I've no doubt at all that it's a wonderfully good movement." Even the Mathewsons' son, Christy Jr., was written about in newspaper stories with headlines such as "America's Proudest Boy."

As the attention grew, Jane tried to keep life at home on an even keel. From their top-floor apartment at St. Nicholas Place and 155th Street, she could keep track of Giants games by watching the Polo Grounds scoreboard, and "as soon as the game reached the seventh inning, I knew it was time to put on my potatoes."

Today, the celebrity of athletes often transcends athletics. That was less frequently the case in Mathewson's day, but he was smart enough to recognize the value of his popular appeal. He was featured in magazine and newspaper advertisements endorsing products such as Coca-Cola ("He's proof of its wholesomeness"), Blauvelt sweaters, and Tuxedo pipe tobacco. He also agreed to lend his name to the marketing of the "Christy Mathewson Parlor Baseball Game," for which he was paid two cents for every game sold, with an advance royalty of $1,000.

He was a valuable commodity to advertisers because, according to one writer, "Mathewson to boy and man is a name linked inseparably to clean living. His life is an open book whose pages tell a simple story of good habits, manliness, honesty, and the possession of will power. In America's greatest city the popular hero of hundreds of thousands; in the midst of all the temptations of teeming masses, Mathewson has stood a forceful example of self-respect and one of the finest specimens of manhood coupled with athletic prowess."

This was a consistent theme in contemporary appraisals of Mathewson and other athletes. "Manly" and "manhood" were used frequently, and references that would be considered sexist today were then treated as high praise. Part of the athlete's role was to serve as a champion of masculinity.

To earn extra money and keep himself busy when he wasn't playing ball, Mathewson went into the insurance business, opening an office on Vesey Street in Manhattan's financial district. The letterhead for "Christy Mathewson, Insurance" proclaimed, "I represent the strongest companies in all branches of insurance." Among his clients were major league team owners. In correspondence with Garry Herrmann, president of the Cincinnati club, Mathewson crisply described a policy that would cover the Cincinnati team if a disaster were to occur: "If 25 men are insured . . . and the special car should be derailed and every one killed, the company would pay you $250,000." In a later letter, he recommended to Herrmann "a cheaper form of accident policy excluding coverage on the field, which has met with the approval of several owners."

Mathewson knew that his pitching arm would last only so long, so he contemplated life after baseball. He continued to think about going into forestry, and told a reporter that he believed "the care of the forests is becoming more and more important every year in the United States, and it will not be long before the settled states of the North and East will have their corps of foresters."

In an article for *Baseball Magazine*, he touted the possibilities offered by the game to a young man "as a profession and as a steppingstone to something else later in life." He added that a ballplayer, during his playing days, "can have learned some other profession. He can have saved up quite a bit of money and have a thriving business already under way when he throws down his glove for the last time. He is a shrewd businessman who uses his baseball proficiency to get hold of money to invest advantageously. . . . By the time one is ready to give up the diamond, if he has grasped his opportunities, he is prepared to take up extended business interests of his own."

His pragmatic view of baseball as steppingstone reflected his realistic appraisal of what might lie ahead. Even the most grizzled major league veterans generally ended their careers before they were forty. The die-hards could find some small-time professional league in which to play a few years longer, but many ballplayers ended up as salesmen or bartenders or in some other middle-class drudgery. Mathewson's goals were higher. He intended to keep making lots of money, and baseball would pave the way for that, just as it had opened doors in his insurance business. He brought a white-collar perspective to the blue-collar world of professional sports.

One writer who visited Mathewson in his insurance office observed, "When you see him behind a roll-top you can hardly make yourself remember he is a ballplayer." He reported that "it is whispered in business circles that Christy is doing exceedingly well." The reason for his success, said the reporter, was that Mathewson "talks like a Harvard graduate, looks like an actor, acts like a businessman, and impresses you as an all-round gentleman."

He also found time to enjoy himself. He liked working with young ballplayers, and he volunteered as a coach. He spent time with the West Point team, helping the cadets while keeping himself in shape. One day at West Point his constant emphasis on precision led to a challenge: Could he throw twenty consecutive pitches, including five fade-aways, to exactly the same spot?

He was hesitant until the cadets offered twelve-to-one odds that he couldn't do it. He then bet fifty dollars on himself.

The cadet catcher squatted behind the plate, holding his mitt with both hands on his knee. Mathewson put every pitch, including the fade-aways, directly into the unmoving pocket. He happily walked away with his $600.

Despite his straight-arrow image, Mathewson was not above such hustling. He loved to gamble on tests of his own skill. He put his "card-index" brain to work at checkers and would play several opponents simultaneously. Sometimes he would do it blindfolded, with someone telling him the numbers of the squares of his opponents' moves. He almost always won. He became the second vice president of the American Checkers Association, and he had a copy of a checkers strategy book that he annotated, sometimes challenging the author's conclusions.

He used the same memory skills as a poker and bridge player, particularly during long train trips with the team. In one poker game he cleaned out a teammate, despite McGraw's order to keep the limit low. McGraw fined Mathewson $500 but didn't penalize any of the other players. He told his star pitcher, "They look up to you, and besides, you knew better." Mathewson accepted the fine with good grace.

His teammates knew that the real Mathewson was not as pure as the image. Years later, pitcher Rube Marquard recalled that Mathewson "loved to gamble. If you had a dollar in your pocket, he would never be satisfied until he got that dollar from you."

He was also a devoted golfer, shooting in the mid-70s, despite McGraw's worry that the game would distract his pitcher. On road trips, Mathewson took along a big trunk, hiding his clubs under his clothes. One morning in Pittsburgh, after beating the Pirates the previous day, Mathewson told his teammate Larry Doyle that he was heading for the golf course, but if McGraw should ask for him, "Tell him I went shopping."

Mathewson got in his eighteen holes that morning, but in the afternoon he was unexpectedly summoned to pitch in relief. The Pirates hit him hard, and afterwards McGraw learned where Mathewson had been before the game. Furious, McGraw called a team meeting, fined Mathewson a hundred dollars, and berated the Giants: "I want to know right now, which is it going to be, baseball or golf? I want every man to make his choice. How about you, Mathewson? Which is it going to be?" Doyle said that Mathewson didn't answer. "He just paid the fine and went on playing golf."

Off the field, Mathewson had few close friends on the team, but he always liked his first catcher, Frank Bowerman. In the off-season he would visit Bowerman at his home in Romeo, Michigan, and they'd go deer hunting. Bowerman once cajoled Mathewson into pitching for the local amateur team. Local legend has it that Mathewson lost that game, but another version says that he shut out the locals' opponents. Take your pick.

Beginning in 1910, Mathewson wrote a series of baseball novels for children that mixed game narrative with subplots involving honest and ambitious young men working their way up in the world.

For these novels and his nonfiction baseball book, *Pitching in a Pinch*, Mathewson worked with *New York Herald* sportswriter John Wheeler. Years later, Wheeler told writer Roger Kahn that most of the work was Mathewson's own. "I was at most Matty's editor or rewrite man," said Wheeler. "He knew how to write and his reading was voracious. He liked the essays of Charles Lamb and studies of psychology. The psychology of pitching? Sure. But more than that. Matty liked to read William James. His favorite novelist was Victor Hugo. I think Matty was the only major leaguer of his era who had read all of *Les Miserables*. He read it two or three times."

When Mathewson decided to embark on another writing venture, a newspaper column about baseball, his editor wanted to assign a ghostwriter because he was afraid the pitcher would not have time to do the pieces on his own. Mathewson replied: "Nobody has ever done my work for me so far. I'll manage."

Exactly how much was written by Mathewson and how much was written by Wheeler can be debated. Granted, these books are not great literature, but they have the flow and polish of a professional writer's work. Mathewson undoubtedly provided the pitching tips scattered through the stories, and he probably wrote the game descriptions, but Wheeler may have contributed to devising the plots and cranking out the dialogue. The principles of sportsmanship defined in the books, however, are clearly Mathewson's own.

Read today, these books are interesting as period pieces. The first, *Won in the Ninth*, describes a college team whose players have remarkably familiar names: Hal Case, Hans Hagner, Joe Brinker, Johnny Everson, Ty (short for "tyrant") Robb, and others. Hagner was "a bowlegged and awkward-looking German," like Honus Wagner, and one opposing pitcher, "Miner" Black, had lost two fingers in a mining accident and was able to put a special curve on the ball, much like Three-Finger Brown, who pitched against Mathewson in many memorable games.

Three of the other books, *Pitcher Pollock, Catcher Craig* and *First Base Faulkner*, are set in Amesville, Ohio, where the residents are always ready to rally behind their high school's ball club. The heroes of the stories are boys who not only triumph on the playing field but also devote themselves with Horatio Alger zeal to improving their modest financial circumstances by working in hardware stores or managing newsstands. They are admired for their "pluck and industry," and one is singled out for his "quiet, contained manner, his cheerfulness, and his unfailing good nature," all Mathewson-like qualities. The adults are supportive and offer vague but inspiring advice: "It's the boy who does his best all the time that won't stay down, son."

Pitchers are praised for the economy of their windups and are reminded that "control's the thing." They are cited for their ability to read batters' minds: "Some of them just seemed to know what the batter was thinking and what he was looking for. Yes, sir, there's a lot more to it than just pitching the ball." Catchers are also extolled: "It's funny about catchers. Their job is the pivotal one on the team and yet they don't get half the credit they deserve. . . . If I had to build up a ball team I'd start in by finding a good catcher, if I could." All that sounds very much like Mathewson speaking.

The last of the Mathewson books, *Second Base Sloan*, published in 1916, is different in its setting and characters. The story borrows some elements from *Huckleberry Finn* as Wayne Sloan runs away from his abusive stepfather in Georgia, accompanied by Junius Bartus Bartow Tasker, his African-American companion. The two teenagers ride the rails to Pennsylvania, where they find work and where Wayne eventually lands a spot on a minor league baseball team. Both boys exhibit persistence during hard times, and Junius—though depicted mostly as caricature—makes some sharp observations about racial hypocrisy in the supposedly enlightened North.

These observations are followed, however, by the comment that Wayne had been brought up in Georgia "in the firm conviction that the Negro was an inferior race." Then the voice of the author intrudes: "Whether he was right or wrong I don't pretend to know." When Wayne makes good, he tells Junius to give up his job as a hotel bellhop and become his personal servant. Wayne says, "We're going to live like white folks again."

Mathewson never publicly addressed race issues, and the remark in *Second Base Sloan*, so offensive today, would not have generated much comment at the time. Many years would pass before baseball became integrated. McGraw once tried to add a black player to the Giants by claiming he was a Native American, but he was quickly found out and the player had to leave the team.

Mathewson's books, along with Frank Chance's 1910 novel, *The*

Bride and the Pennant (probably ghostwritten by sportswriter Hugh Fullerton), were the first to link a real ballplayer to fictional sports stories. This genre, in which the player often did little more than rent out the use of his name, continued with "authors" including Babe Ruth (*The Home Run King*) and Willie Mays (*Danger in Center Field*). Only a few player-writers, such as former minor leaguer Zane Grey, brought genuine literary skills to their books.

Baseball has a lengthy history in fiction. Probably the first reference to baseball in a novel is in Jane Austen's *Northanger Abbey*, completed in 1799, in which heroine Catherine Morland at age fourteen preferred "base ball," among other athletic pursuits, to books. There is no telling exactly what this game was. Austen distinguishes it from cricket, which she mentions separately, but says nothing further about it. It must have been just one of the many ancestors of the American sport.

Beginning in the 1890s, tales of athletic derring-do became extremely popular in the Frank and Dick Merriwell series by Gilbert Patten, who was using the pen name of Burt L. Standish. Hundreds of Merriwell stories appeared in *Tip Top Weekly* magazine and were then anthologized in paperback volumes. Street & Smith publishers touted their series by claiming that "a half million enthusiastic followers of the Merriwell brothers will attest the unfailing interest and wholesomeness of these adventures of two lads of high ideals."

The Merriwell baseball books usually had one or both of the Merriwells foiling an array of villains as well as excelling on the diamond. These tales, said the publisher, "are extremely high in moral tone, and cannot fail to be of immense benefit to every boy who reads them. [They possess] the splendid quality of firing a boy's ambition to become a good athlete, in order that he may develop into a strong, vigorous, right-thinking man."

The Merriwells were classic heroes, skilled and resolute. In one of the books, the reader is reminded that "the name of Frank Merriwell was synonymous with all that was noble and manly." These stories had an enormous following; readers were delighted to find athlete-heroes to embrace.

The Mathewson books—uplifting and sometimes cautionary in their advice to young readers—reflected contemporary culture and standards. They include praise for athletics as a social equalizer: "There is nothing like athletics to put boys on a common ground, and a fellow was always welcome to show what he could do." In *Won in the Ninth*, participation in college sports is justified with the argument that "the pursuit of athletics in college need not interfere with a fellow's studies, and if you give a boy a well developed body his brain will get the benefit of it."

Catcher Craig includes Mathewson's observations about college athletic scholarships. In the novel a wealthy alumnus tries to recruit Craig to come play baseball for his university, suggesting that a scholarship can be arranged. Craig asks, "But isn't it a good deal like paying a fellow to play for the college, sir?" Despite the alum's protest that "there's nothing like that to it," Craig refuses the offer.

Today universities blithely provide athletic scholarships that sometimes are indeed little more than "paying a fellow to play." Alums and other boosters have given college athletes cash, cars and other gifts, regardless of rules prohibiting such under-the-table deals. Scandals arising from such practices have tainted numerous schools. Catcher Craig, of course, would never have succumbed.

Several of the Mathewson books also present a defense of professional baseball. From *Pitcher Pollock*: "There's a pretty fine, self-respecting lot of men playing professional ball these days." And in *Second Base Sloan*: "Lots of folks think professional baseball is like highway robbery or something. They class professional ballplayers and prize fighters and thugs all together. I guess there was a time when some ballplayers were a roughish lot, but that's gone by. Most of them are just like the rest of us nowadays. A lot of them lead cleaner lives than the folks who knock them."

Mathewson's voice rings clearly in such passages. He was always conscious of his mother's initial disappointment about his choice of career. In his fictional ballplayers' defense of the game, you can hear Christy making his case to his mother.

The books link noble amateurism and respectable professionalism. Professionals, says *Won in the Ninth*, "like to play the game for the fun there is in it as much as the profit. They like it for the thrilling situations and the excitement. They love to see the big crowds, and when the stands are filled and they have to let the crowd out on the field they play their best and are just as anxious to win every game" as they were when they played amateur ball. The boys from Amesville and their brethren in the other books are told by their fans, if not always by their parents, that pro ball is something worth aspiring to. A friend tells Wayne in *Second Base Sloan*, "You can be a professional ballplayer now and be a gentleman, too."

This is part of Christy Mathewson's lasting impact on the game. His public persona was that of ballplayer *and* gentleman. The two were no longer mutually exclusive.

As the success of Mathewson's books showed, baseball novels had a big audience among young readers. To capitalize on this, Ernest Stratemeyer, writing as Lester Chadwick, started the fourteen-book *Baseball Joe* series in 1912. Joe begins on his local team, stars at prep school and college, rips through the minor leagues, and becomes a major league hero with the Cardinals and Giants. As the Giants' star pitcher, he strikes out 27 Cubs to win the pennant in *Baseball Joe, Pitching Wizard*, the final volume of the series.

Baseball Joe is a slightly disguised Christy Mathewson. Even Joe's last name, Matson, is an abbreviation of Mathewson. Joe's mother, like Mathewson's, wanted her son to become a clergyman rather than a ballplayer. She reconciles herself to his choice of career when she realizes her son is not only successful, but also proves to be "a ballplayer and at the same time an upright, moral man."

After establishing himself as a star athlete at college, Joe leaves school to become a pro, just as Mathewson did. Young Joe has young Christy's determination: "I may not make good," says Joe, "but I'm going to try awfully hard."

In *Baseball Joe on the Giants*, published in 1916, Matson is managed by a fictional version of John McGraw—McRae—who is "as foxy as they make them." Joe is patterned after Mathewson, but when he joins the Giants, another incarnation of Mathewson is already there. Matson's New York teammate is Hughson, "the most famous pitcher in the game." McRae calls him "one of the finest men that ever stepped in shoe leather." Joe responds: "Isn't he a prince? You don't know whether to admire him most as a man or player." Hughson is similarly admiring of Matson, so the two versions of Mathewson get along well.

Besides their mutual esteem and similar pitching skill, the principal link between Baseball Joe and Mathewson is their shared philosophy of sport. *Baseball Joe at Yale* contains this passage: "Doesn't playing at an athletic game fit one to play in life? It isn't always the winning that counts, but the spirit of fair play, the love for the square deal, the respect for a worthy foe, and the determination not to give up until you are fairly beaten—all these things count for much." Baseball fans associated this concept of sportsmanship with Mathewson, and the public sensed that the integrity of the game was growing stronger. When scandal erupted about an individual player's behavior—or worse, about corruption of the game itself caused by partnerships between players and gamblers—there was no longer just an accepting shrug, but great disappointment—"Say it ain't so"—that the ideal had been betrayed.

Baseball novels had their share of gamblers and other villains, and so did Mathewson's one effort as a playwright. He joined writer Rida Johnson Young as coauthor of *The Girl and the Pennant*, a comedy of "youth, romance, and baseball" that appeared at New York's Lyric

Theater in 1913. *Theater* magazine called the play "a very ingenuous entertainment." It was the story of a young woman who inherits a baseball team after the death of her father, who had "played the game for the game's sake." She determines to win the pennant to honor him, but the manager wants to lose so he and another scoundrel can buy the team at a bargain price.

The game that will decide the pennant takes place off stage, but it is described fully on a large scoreboard and by players who appear on stage after they have been ejected from the game by the umpire. During the last inning, the owner takes over from her crooked manager, calmly orders a double-steal, and inserts an unlikely pinch hitter who, of course, delivers the game winner. In the final scene, pinch hitter and owner become engaged. Great stuff.

In *The Girl and the Pennant*, two of the main characters are brothers who are teammates. Christy Mathewson was in the same position when his brother Henry joined the Giants in 1906. Henry was six years younger than Christy, and he came to the Giants after pitching for semipro teams in Pennsylvania. Christy told reporters that his brother "has as much speed as I had when I broke into the game, and he has control and a splendid assortment of curves. All he wants is experience, and with that I am sure he will develop into a star."

McGraw, however, was unimpressed. At the end of the season, he used Henry for one uneventful inning in relief of Christy, and then let him pitch a complete game in which he walked fourteen while losing 7-1.

Henry made a one-inning appearance in 1907, and his big league career was over. McGraw didn't think he had enough talent to merit a spot on the Giants' roster. He played in the minors briefly and was then diagnosed with tuberculosis. He lived in Arizona for a while, and then came back to Factoryville, where he died in 1917 at age thirty.

An even sadder story is that of Christy's other brother, Nicholas. Nine years younger than Christy, he was thought by some in Factoryville to be the best pitcher in the family, with a fastball that surpassed his oldest brother's. While pitching a game in Scranton, he attracted the attention of Detroit manager Hughie Jennings, who offered him a $3,000 contract if the Mathewsons would let him go to Detroit. Although Jennings promised not to "work him hard," Gilbert and Minerva said no. They wanted their eighteen-year-old to go to college, and only after that consider a baseball career.

Nick had been recruited by Lafayette College in Easton, Pennsylvania, which wanted him for its baseball team. He started classes at Lafayette but came home during his first semester, home-sick and fighting what seemed to be a minor ailment. (One Factoryville friend claimed Nick had been diagnosed with the first stages of tuberculosis, but no family member ever confirmed this.) His mood swung back and forth between depression about falling behind in his studies and happiness about a planned vacation with friends.

On a brisk January day in 1909, he climbed into the hayloft in the barn behind the house, scrawled a farewell note, and fired a bullet into his brain. Christy was visiting his parents at the time and found the body.

Despite his sorrow, Christy kept working and kept his sadness to himself. His father once talked briefly with a journalist about Nick's death, but the Mathewson family generally kept private matters pri- vate. Even many years later, Jane would not discuss Christy's brothers.

Mathewson's stoicism about personal tragedy was another aspect of the self-control he demonstrated at the ballpark. John McGraw's on-field explosions were the norm in professional baseball, and play-ers were still considered brawlers. Mathewson, however, remained above the fray, a model of noble sportsmanship. The contrast was striking, and the public was gravitating to the kind of baseball he represented. Responsibility and maturity were respected as the nation moved through the first years of what was to become the American century, and Mathewson reflected this new ideal. His star would continue to rise.

FOUR

Star Power

New York American REPORTER KATE CAREW was thoroughly charmed. She was not a baseball fan, but this Christy Mathewson . . . he was something.

She told her readers, "He's the greatest matinee idol of our time, his eyes ever so blue, and his hair ever so yellow, and his cheeks ever so red, and I thought of Phoebus, the sun god, and of a young Viking with a two-handed sword." Carew went on to describe walking with Mathewson after interviewing him and "running the gauntlet of many matinee girls, who commented agitatedly on the perfections of their hero." She asked him if he found such popularity inconvenient. "No, I don't mind it a bit," he answered. She asked if he received notes from his female admirers. "Oh, yes," he said, "my wife answers those."

Mathewson put his matinee idol assets to work, becoming one of the many ballplayers to step—or tapdance—onto the vaudeville stage. The allure was more than just the glamour of showbiz. Well-known athletes could make upwards of $2,000 a week—a year's baseball salary for a few weeks of work. As Minnie Marx, mother of Groucho and his brothers, put it, "Where else can people who don't know anything make so much money?"

Boxers made up the largest contingent of athletes in vaudeville, with baseball players ranking second. Among the fighters who went on stage were John L. Sullivan, Jack Johnson, Jack Dempsey, and Jess Willard. Many did monologues about the boxing world; others, more ambitious, acted in skits. A few theaters featured Dutch boxer Joop Leit, who was known for singing bits of opera in the ring after knocking out an opponent. When he brought his singing to the vaudeville stage, he won more laughter than cheers.

One of the first baseball acts to attract wide attention featured Giants outfielder Mike Donlin and his wife, singer-comedienne Mabel Hite, whose skits included "Stealing Home." Donlin skipped the 1907 baseball season to manage Hite and pursue his own theatrical career. He returned to the Giants in 1908, hit .334, and then promptly jumped ship again. When Mabel died in 1913, he lost his taste for performing, and a sympathetic John McGraw brought him back to the Giants as a pinch hitter.

Mathewson had little enthusiasm for plunging into the flashy excesses of show business, but the money was good, and in 1910 he and his catcher Chief Meyers toured together in "Curves," a sketch written by sportswriter Bozeman Bulger. As the act traveled across the country, Mathewson often found a crowd of admiring boys gathered by the stage door, hoping to get a glimpse of their hero. Always a soft touch, he would instruct the theater manager to let all the boys in and charge their tickets to him.

Although he was comfortable pitching in front of tens of thousands, Mathewson had to battle stage fright every time he did his act. When he was offered even more money to do another tour the next winter, he turned it down.

John McGraw had no problems with stage fright and happily basked in the footlights as he presented a monologue, "Inside Baseball" (also largely written by Bulger), for which he was paid $3,000 a week. It ran for fifteen weeks. McGraw was advertised as baseball's best storyteller, who would "relate a series of humorous incidents and explain the workings of a major league ball team." The audience was promised a look at McGraw's "largest and finest collection of photographs of historic and decisive plays," which were reproduced on slides to illustrate his spiel. He strutted back and forth across the stage, jabbing his finger at the audience as if instructing his players.

Ballplayers continued to appear on stage for years to come. Ty Cobb, Joe Tinker, Germany Schaefer, and later Babe Ruth and Waite Hoyt, whose father had been a minstrel singer, all had vaudeville acts. Sports and show business had a lot in common, and now that athletes were celebrities they moved back and forth between the playing field and the stage.

Mathewson also tried his hand at movies, appearing in several productions of the Universal Film Company, an ancestor of today's Universal Studios. A typical film was *The Umpire*, in which Mathewson played himself in a fictional situation. He and his teammate Eddie compete for the attentions of the same young woman, the charming Lillian. How will she decide between her suitors? She turns to her father, a former big league catcher.

"I've got it! Let them play a game of baseball! Let each of them be on different sides! Marry the man who wins the game!"

Of course!

After a dramatic game and a display of selfless sportsmanship by Christy, his pal prevails. But Lillian loves Christy.

"Oh, Christy! I've got to marry him—but, oh, why couldn't you have won?"

"I lost, and we've got to play the game, little girl."

How sad! But Eddie has overheard, and he steps aside. True love and Christy prevail in the end.

Mathewson made a number of films, with titles such as *Love and Baseball*. Other players also tried movies. Ty Cobb starred in *Somewhere in Georgia*, in which he is kidnapped and forced to ride a mule to get to the game at the crucial moment. (One critic called it "absolutely the worst movie I've ever seen.") Giants outfielder Mike Donlin, on the heels of his vaudeville success, made a number of movies, including *Right Off the Bat*, which also featured John McGraw.

Vaudeville, however, remained the most popular medium for ballplayer-actors. Their principal venue was the Victoria Theater, at Forty-second Street and Seventh Avenue. It seated 1,250 and the average ticket cost a dollar. One of vaudeville's biggest moneymakers, it grossed $20 million by the time it closed in 1915, after operating for about sixteen years. The Victoria was run with great flair by Willie Hammerstein, father of lyricist Oscar Hammerstein II. It was a raucous place, and Hammerstein proudly proclaimed, "The bar is never closed."

Hammerstein aggressively searched for acts, famous and infamous, that would put customers in the seats. He regularly booked women who had become celebrities by shooting their boyfriends (two of whom he billed as "The Shooting Stars") or by suing prominent dandies for breach of promise. Among his performers was Jimmy Bell, a boy tenor who sang while standing on one foot and sometimes with one eye closed—"to make it harder," he said. There was also a man with a seventeen-foot beard, and a woman named Sober Sue; nobody—not even the comedians Hammerstein hired to tempt her—could make her laugh. (Her sober mien was actually the product of paralyzed facial muscles.) Among the Victoria's musical acts was Flossie Crane, "the girl from Coney Island," who could switch her voice from baritone to soprano in mid-song.

At another of his vaudeville theaters, the Manhattan Opera House, Hammerstein presented attractions such as Polaire, a Parisian actress who, according to the *Times*, "frankly admits that she's the ugliest woman in the world."

And then there was Machnow, a 9'2" Russian who was a crowd-pleaser even though he stood on the stage and did nothing. In a typical publicity stunt, Hammerstein arranged to have Machnow arrested for walking on the grass in Central Park. He couldn't fit into the police wagon, which made for great newspaper photos.

In the relentless competition for patrons, Hammerstein combined inventiveness with a casual attitude toward truth in advertising. On hot summer days he posted a sign saying that it was just 70 degrees inside his theater, and invited those who doubted him to check the large thermometer in the lobby. The thermometer verified Hammerstein's claim, but he made sure no one saw the block of ice hidden beneath it. He also heated the elevator that took patrons to the theater's glass-covered roof garden, so when they got there it seemed relatively cool.

The razzmatazz of the Victoria and other theaters fostered a boom in the area around Broadway and Forty-second Street. Lavishly designed restaurants, known as "lobster palaces," attracted a clientele of show business and sports figures. Louis Martin's, Rector's, Churchill's, and others offered their lobsters and "hot bird and cold bottle" dinners late into the night. When ballroom dancing was at its peak between 1912 and 1916, these restaurants featured the likes of Vernon and Irene Castle on their dance floors.

This corner of New York life was long on dazzle and short on sleep. Despite his occasional theatrical endeavors, Mathewson stayed only on the edges of this world. He and Jane might see a play and then dine at Delmonico's, but their nights on the town were rarely wilder than that.

At one point he was offered a chance at some easy money by lending his name to a Broadway bar. All he had to do was let it be called "Christy Mathewson's" and show up for ten minutes once or twice a week. He was told he could make thousands of dollars a year from the venture. He turned it down, later telling his mother, "If I had to make money that way I wouldn't want any."

Some of his teammates, however, felt much more comfortable liv-

ing the high life. None of them loved the spotlight more than Rube
Marquard.

Marquard had no doubt that he was ready for the big leagues and
Broadway. John McGraw purchased his contract in 1908 from the
Indianapolis minor league team for the then-grand sum of $11,000,
and assigned Mathewson to make sure the investment paid off.
Matty's pitching lessons helped; in three consecutive seasons
Marquard won more than 20 games, and in 1912 he won 19 straight.
Mathewson's lectures about work ethic had less effect.

Fascinated by the glitter of New York, Marquard tried his hand at
vaudeville, doing baseball-related song-and-dance routines. He was
quite good at it. His voice was decent, he was a graceful dancer and he
possessed a combination of charm and confidence that appealed to
audiences. He made his stage debut in 1911, and the following year,
soon after the World Series (which the Giants lost to Boston),
Marquard appeared at the Victoria in *Breaking the Record, or The 19th
Straight*. A featured song was "The Marquard Glide," sung by his
costar, Blossom Seeley, a well known vaudevillian who was married to
her manager, former actor Joe Kane.

A romance between Marquard and Seeley soon caught fire, as did
Kane's temper. The New York press jumped on the story when
Marquard escorted Seeley to the courthouse so she could file a com-
plaint against her husband.

"Joe abused me, assaulted me, threw mirrors at me, cut my
clothes, beat me with his fists, and [was] waving a revolver and saying he was going to shoot me on the stage."

Marquard, said a news report, was smiling as she told her story.
He then informed reporters that he was Seeley's new manager. The
news item also noted that Seeley "had left her former abode in the
Hotel Hermitage and had gone to live at the Endicott. Marquard also
lives at the Endicott."

Kane responded by filing a criminal complaint against Marquard, charging him with adultery, which at the time could lead to a year in jail. Marquard and Seeley paid no attention to the angry husband and went to Atlantic City for a few days. Kane and private detectives he had hired tracked them to their hotel room and forced them to exit down a fire escape and leave town. The public loved the sensational chase. The *New York American* headlined the story "Marquard Fleeing, Blossom With Him."

Kane filed an alienation of affection suit, which was settled for $4,000 shortly after he and Seeley were divorced. While all this was going on, the vaudeville act "Marquard and Seeley" embarked on a successful national tour. The two were married in March of 1913.

The Sporting News sniffed that the couple's large and appreciative audiences were merely a byproduct of the scandal, and that Marquard deserved to be "pulled into oblivion." When Marquard tried to use his theatrical success as leverage to get a big raise from the Giants, McGraw went public with his criticism of his pitcher: "Marquard hasn't done himself or the New York club any good by his actions this winter. . . . It is unfortunate that his conduct has made it unpleas-ant for all the rest of us on the team. Let him get all the free advertis-ing he can, but let him use some sense in choosing his methods."

Marquard and Seeley continued their off-season touring, appear-ing in such successes as *The Suffragette Pitcher*. Seeley played the pitcher while Marquard was the stay-at-home husband who, dressed in women's clothing, was added to Seeley's baseball team. Their mar-riage survived that story line, but before long the conflicting demands of baseball and the stage became too much, and they divorced in 1920. Marquard pitched until 1925 and ended up in the Hall of Fame. Seeley kept performing into the television era and appeared on *The Ed Sullivan Show* when she was in her late sixties.

Any reluctance to cheer what might once have been dismissed as "friv-olous" diversions was vanishing as new social standards took hold. Mark Sullivan, a journalist and lively chronicler of the century's first decades, wrote: "Conventions which had been respected, traditions that had been revered, codes that had been obeyed almost as precepts of religion, had been undermined or had disappeared. In their place had come new ways, new attitudes of mind, new manners."

The environment in which Mathewson and the Giants performed was also changing. New York was America's great metropolis, and as such helped shape the culture of the entire nation. It was, however, unlike urban centers elsewhere in the world because, Sullivan wrote, it "was made up mainly of peoples different from the country whose culture it modified." According to the 1910 census, 79 percent of New York's approximately five million residents had been born abroad or were the children of immigrants. New York, said Sullivan, was the largest Italian city in the world, the largest Jewish city in the world, and offered newspapers in twenty-three languages.

In 1907, the *Jewish Daily Forward* published an explanation of baseball's fundamentals, accompanied by a diagram of the Polo Grounds. But most adult immigrants had little use for sports because they spent their time in the ceaseless task of providing for their families. What few extra hours they had were mostly devoted to religious or other cultural traditions.

Baseball did, however, reach the newcomers through their children. Schools and recreational programs used baseball to teach "American ideas and ideals." Journalist Hugh Fullerton called baseball "the greatest single force working for Americanization. No other game appeals so much to the foreign-born youngsters and nothing, not even the schools, teaches the American spirit so quickly, or inculcates the idea of sportsmanship or fair play as thoroughly."

Mathewson had pitched for the Scranton, Pennsylvania, YMCA team when he was a teenager, and now the Y and settlement houses organized baseball teams to engage children from immigrant and other low-income families in "healthful" activities. New York's Public Schools Athletic League, founded in 1903, encouraged children in tenement districts to join athletic teams that would foster "fairness, cheerfulness, pluck, and skill—the true sportsmanlike spirit of honorable competition."

During a visit to the New York Juvenile Asylum in Dobbs Ferry, Mathewson told the 550 boys, "I might lecture to you about control being the big thing in life." Instead, he talked about the fine points of pitching. The *Times* praised his reluctance to moralize and said "his oratory is under as perfect control as his valuable right arm." Mathewson invited the boys to come to the Polo Grounds, and the reformatory's superintendent promised to charter a train and bring them.

In Chicago, Jane Addams of Hull House noted that local baseball games were "attended by thousands of men and boys." During the noon hour, she wrote, "all the employees of a city factory gather in the nearest vacant lot to cheer their own home team in its practice for the next game with the nine of a neighboring manufacturing establishment, and on a Saturday afternoon the entire male population of the city betakes itself to the baseball field."

Addams praised baseball as an alternative to the pernicious influence of popular theater and films, especially on boys who took the onstage stories seriously. In a case similar to those cited by today's critics of violent movies and television shows, Addams told of three young boys who were so moved by a theatrical depiction of a Wild West stagecoach holdup that they acquired a revolver and a rope and tried to rob a milkman. Fortunately, his rearing horse foiled the would-be outlaws.

Baseball was seen by Addams as a constructive social equalizer. At a game, she said, "the enormous crowd of cheering men and boys are talkative, good-natured, full of holiday spirit, and absolutely released from the grind of life. . . . He does not call the stranger who sits next to him 'brother' but he unconsciously embraces him in an overwhelming outburst of kindly feeling when the favorite player makes a home run. Does this not contain a suggestion of the undoubted power of public recreation to bring together all classes of a community in the modern city unhappily so full of devices for keeping men apart?"

Scholar Steven Riess echoed Addams, observing that "baseball fostered social integration by promoting acculturation and hometown pride, by teaching respect for authority, and by giving factory workers much-needed exercise and diversion." Baseball was also promoted as a thoroughly democratic enterprise, with players making the big leagues based solely on merit.

This, of course, was simply untrue. As the African-American experience in baseball proved, merit was irrelevant if your skin wasn't white. Players from other ethnic groups also encountered discrimination that obstructed their path to the major leagues.

Occasionally, teams such as the Giants acquired players who might appeal to ethnic blocs within the city. An example was Moe Solomon, a New York–born minor league slugger who was known as "the rabbi of swat." McGraw brought Solomon to the Giants, but his big league career consisted of just two games (in which he went 3 for 8).

At the ballparks, then as now, fans were not seated in a democratic mass, but rather according to how much they paid for their tickets. Wealthy fans and factory workers may have rooted for the same teams and players, but they did not mix in major league grandstands. Those with money could sit in shaded seats, while others baked in the bleachers. As new stadiums were built and old ones expanded, the great majority of seats were the more expensive ones. Baseball clubs were more concerned with maximizing profits than attracting lower-income fans. That remains true today.

Nevertheless, fans of all social classes rooted for the home team as an expression of local pride. For the newest Americans, allegiance to a team was part of forging their American identity. They wanted to *belong*, to have something in common with others in their community. They may have had trouble with the language and customs of this new place, but like everyone else they could cheer for their home team and heap abuse on the visitors.

Rooting for individual players was another part of forging a common identity. A star such as Mathewson attracted these fans not just because of his superb skills on the field, but also because he could be viewed by the first- or second-generation citizen as the model American—not like us, but someone for us to emulate as we make this new country truly our home. Just look at him: handsome, skilled, admired; a champion at the most American of games.

The newcomers wanted accessible heroes, and Matty filled the role. He could be cheered in person at the ballpark, and his exploits could be followed in the press and praised in neighborhood conversation. He was personally remote, as celebrities always are, but because his game was part of daily life on the neighborhood streets, he seemed closer. He became *theirs*.

The President of the United States was speaking about a subject close to his heart when he told his audience at the Southern Hotel in St. Louis: "The game of baseball is a clean, straight game, and it summons to its presence everybody who enjoys clean, straight athletics. It furnishes amusement to thousands and thousands. I like to go for two reasons: first, because I enjoy myself and second, because if by the presence of the chief magistrate such a healthy amusement can be encouraged, I want to encourage it."

President William Howard Taft then cut his speech short and rushed out of the hotel. He went directly to the ballpark to see his hometown's Cincinnati Reds play the Cardinals. He stayed for just two innings—the Cardinals outscored the Reds 12-0 during that time—and then departed for St. Louis's other major league park, where the American League Browns were hosting Cleveland. He wanted to see Cy Young, who was nearing the end of his career and was pitching for Cleveland that day.

Taft had been an amateur ballplayer himself while growing up in

Cincinnati and studying at Yale, and he did not let being the country's chief executive dilute his devotion to baseball. During his presidential travels, he frequently arranged his schedule so he could stop by the local ballpark. His enthusiasm for baseball was so well known that his appearances at games were touted in advance. While visiting Pittsburgh in May 1910, the president found placards on street cars saying, "Go see Taft at the ball game." He complained, "That is very near the limit when they advertise the president as the chief attraction at a ball game."

Taft began the tradition of the president throwing out the first ball on the season's opening day. Taft was a fan of Washington pitcher Walter Johnson, and that brought him to the Washington stadium on April 14, 1910, joined by Vice President James Sherman, another baseball fan. Team owner Thomas Noyes found a chair suitable for the 300-plus-pound Taft and asked him to begin the season with a presidential toss. (The first nonpresidential celebrity to perform this ceremony in Washington had been Admiral George Dewey, the hero of Manila Bay, in 1901.) Johnson caught the ball—on a hop—and proceeded to pitch a shutout. The next day he sent the ball to the White House for a presidential signature. Taft inscribed it, "To Walter Johnson, with the hope that he may continue to be as formidable as in yesterday's game."

Taft was a dedicated public servant who had worked closely with Theodore Roosevelt as governor of the Philippines and secretary of war. Roosevelt had pledged not to seek reelection in 1908, and he secured the nomination for his protégé Taft, who went on to easily defeat Democrat William Jennings Bryan.

Despite his victory at the polls, Taft's popularity was shaky. He lacked Roosevelt's political stature and rhetorical flair. Historian Mark Sullivan noted that crowds at rallies failed "to get much more than amiably tolerant about Taft." That left him vulnerable, particularly because the politics of his party and the nation were changing.

The progressive movement was strong, and its adherents demanded that government do more to reform itself and control big business.

Taft was not the best leader for this turbulent time. He told an aide, "When I hear someone say 'Mr. President,' I look around expecting to see Roosevelt." He lacked the political dexterity needed to fashion a new Republican Party that could embrace aspects of progressivism without alienating its old-guard core. Perhaps Roosevelt could have done so, but the task would have been difficult even for him. Forces of change tugged at the Republicans, pulling the party this way and that and finally tearing it apart. Roosevelt and Taft split, and when Taft held on to the party's 1912 nomination, Roosevelt ran anyway, the candidate of the Progressive, or Bull Moose, Party. His doing so ensured Taft's defeat.

After his presidency, Taft became chief justice of the U.S. Supreme Court, the only person ever to serve in that job as well as the presidency. He probably would have been happier if he had gone to the Court instead of the White House in the first place, and he certainly would have preferred spending less time on politics and more on baseball. The game was far more stable than politics.

While the political world was in turmoil, Mathewson remained steady. He followed his 37-win 1908 season with a 25-6 record in 1909. His earned run average that year was 1.14, his all-time best. In 1910, he went 27-9; in 1911, 26-13; in 1912, 23-12; in 1913, 25-11. The Giants, who had been without a pennant since 1905, won the league title in 1911, 1912, and 1913, but lost the World Series each year, twice to the Philadelphia Athletics and once to the Boston Red Sox.

Mathewson's personal successes kept pace with those of his team. On May 2, 1910, he pitched a no-hitter against Brooklyn. A press report described it like this: "Flinging with all the skill of a master of his craft, Christy Mathewson—six feet tall, surmounted with a dome full of baseball knowledge—shut out the Brooklyns at Washington

Park yesterday, not allowing the Dodgers to pelt the ball to a single uninhabited spot on the diamond."

Another Mathewson milestone—his 250th career win—had to compete with an even bigger sports story: Jack Johnson's victory over James J. Jeffries for the heavyweight championship. That was front page news, as were stories about people being killed in the race riots around the country that followed Johnson's becoming the first black champion. In New York, reported the *Times*, "Gangs of men and boys formed apparently for the sole purpose of beating up whatever Negroes they could get their hands upon, and in many instances the Negroes retaliated."

In May 1912, on the day of another Mathewson win, the big news was the march up Fifth Avenue of an estimated 9,000 women and 1,000 men supporting women's suffrage. They were watched by many thousands more who "took over every inch of the sidewalk from Washington Square to Carnegie Hall." The *Times* reported that "women young and old, rich and poor, were all banded into a great sisterhood by the cause they hold dear. . . . There were women who work with their heads and women who work with their hands and women who never work at all. And they all marched for suffrage."

On the sports page, the report about Mathewson's victory for the Giants noted that "the suffragette parade kept the crowd [at the Polo Grounds] down to 15,000, but even so, the fighters for the women's cause will be surprised to know that plenty of their sisters passed up the long tramp to see the game."

Mathewson was not invincible. In the first game of a July 4th doubleheader in 1912, he was knocked out of the game after giving up five runs in three innings. When he came back to pitch again the next day, reported the *Times*, "there was a broad grin on the faces of the upstart Brooklyn players."

But he quickly showed them, as the *Times* noted, that "not yet is

Mathewson ready to go to the home for the aged and infirm." He displayed his "back-breaking fade-away, saucy inshoots, deceptive out-hops, a slow ball that hesitated in midair two or three times before reaching the pan, and control which kept the pill under magician-like influence all the while." For good measure, he occasionally produced a fastball "wreathed in smoke."

Unmentioned in news reports was that this was Mathewson's 300th win, a milestone rarely reached by a pitcher. By this point in his career, approaching his thirty-second birthday, Mathewson was thinking even more carefully as he pitched. He had never relied solely on his physical prowess, and McGraw had always believed that Mathewson's intelligence, coupled with his pure skills, had set him above other pitchers. Now Mathewson could reflect that "every year baseball becomes more of a thinking game. Each year the game becomes just a little bit more complicated. Baseball is demanding more and more a better coordination between brain and brawn." By recognizing that and acting on it, Mathewson was able to extend his career.

He knew, however, that success could not be sustained merely by following a brawn-plus-brain formula. There was the heart to consider as well. He wrote: "A person must enjoy playing baseball. He must not go at it as he would seat himself at an office desk at nine in the morning and then keep his eye on the clock until five in the evening. He must like it, must love it, must put his whole soul in it."

Fans continued to gravitate to Matty. One boy from South Carolina sent him fifty cents "for which would you please tell me how to throw your fade-away." Mathewson wrote back with some pitching advice and returned the money. Another young admirer told the pitcher that he was one of his "boosters" and was doing well in school, and asked if Matty would please send him a baseball. The letter reached Mathewson in California during the off-season, so he replied, "I haven't a baseball to send you, but the next time you are at the Polo Grounds, if you will make yourself known to me, I will give you one that has been used in a League game."

In the first years of the twentieth century, the nation was changing—its people, its politics, its power. Mathewson was part of that change. He had helped to bring new legitimacy to baseball, showing that professionalism need not blemish sport. He had established himself as a widely admired public figure, with a life beyond the ballpark that extended from the insurance business to the vaudeville stage. His New York Giants, in their success, displayed a boisterous assertiveness similar to that which Theodore Roosevelt's presidency had brought to politics. Baseball was keeping pace with the times.

Other aspects of national life progressed less steadily. The pale tenure of William Howard Taft left Americans looking for a different kind of chief executive. During the search for a new leader, idealism had particular appeal as a manifestation of noble national purpose. When they selected a new president in 1912, the American people moved in that direction.

FIVE

The Moral Nation

THE GRACE METHODIST EPISCOPAL CHURCH on 104th Street was packed, and the congregation's fervor transcended normal Sunday worship. The World Series was about to begin and the pastor was doing his best to make sure the Lord would be behind the New York Giants.

As they entered the church, parishioners were given photographs of the Giants, and they could also stare at the real thing. Chief Meyers, Fred Snodgrass, Hooks Wiltse, Jim Thorpe, and other players were in the pews that day.

Reverend C. F. Reisner praised certain players as fine examples of Christian manhood. When he named Christy Mathewson, the congregation erupted in cheers. The pastor reminded the Giants' admirers where they were, and for the rest of the service their behavior was more restrained, even if their prayers were directed at upcoming events at the Polo Grounds.

Sharing the pulpit with Reverend Reisner was Dave Fultz, a former major league outfielder who had become president of the ballplayers' union. He spoke about "The Christian Player" and said, "Just as is baseball, so is life a game, and in life we must also run and hit and tally and rally."

Reverend Reisner read letters from notables including the World Series managers, John McGraw and Connie Mack, and two former players, Pennsylvania governor John Tener and evangelist Billy Sunday. After hearing a lot about baseball and virtue, the members of the congregation departed with high hopes for divine intervention on the Giants' behalf.

As it turned out, the Lord was unmoved. The Giants lost the Series to the Athletics in five games.

Baseball and religion, as two dominant elements of American culture, intersected frequently. In 1896, Cardinal James Gibbons of Baltimore endorsed the game. "It is a healthy sport, and since the people of the country generally demand some sporting event for their amusement, I would single this out as the best one to be patronized, and heartily approve of it as a popular pastime."

Sometimes, at levels lower than cardinal, the clergy's interest in baseball caused problems. At a Baptist church in Scranton, Pennsylvania, deacons disapproved of their pastor attending ballgames and asked that he stop doing so. He refused and resigned, but the congregation then voted overwhelmingly to not accept his resignation.

In Middleton, New York, the pastor of the Methodist Episcopal church announced that a baseball game would be one of the attractions at a church picnic. Horrified church elders locked the pastor out of the church and told him that he could no longer preach there. Liberal-minded church members seceded, started a Free Methodist church in a nearby schoolhouse, and hired the baseball-loving pastor to lead them.

After the 1906 World Series, a Chicago minister wrote to White Sox president Charles Comiskey: "It appears to me unfortunate both for myself and my church on this occasion that I was forbidden by my calling to wager upon the outcome. Otherwise I should have won enough to pay off the parish debt."

Some cities banned Sunday baseball, a restriction that teams often chose to ignore. Occasionally, police officers would halt the games and arrest players, ticket-takers, and scorecard-sellers. If the case reached the court of a judge who liked baseball, charges would be dismissed and the defendants told to play ball. In 1904, a New York judge declared Sunday baseball to be legal and added, "If our boys cannot be permitted to go out on Sunday and indulge in a game as innocent as this, then the democracy of the United States is endangered."

That did not settle the issue. Some clergy and others maintained their support for a Sunday ban, and not until 1919 was a state law passed that allowed Sunday ball games in New York City. Proponents of this measure had to overcome opposition from Sabbatarians who denounced the move as opening the door to bolshevism.

As recently as 1998, New York's Cardinal John O'Connor announced that he would boycott Major League baseball because games were played on Good Friday. O'Connor also asked that Little League baseball reinstate its Sunday baseball ban, which had been lifted in 1988. Little League officials declined.

Mathewson was among the small number of players who chose not to play on Sundays. When he first began to play professionally, he promised his mother he would observe the Sabbath. She told a reporter, "There may be some good arguments in favor of Sunday games in some places, but I should not like to see my boy playing on that day, and he knows that." Christy himself said that he had modified his views on the matter, partly because "New York has a much wider horizon than Factoryville. There is much to be said in favor of allowing the laboring man his only opportunity to see a baseball game on Sunday. My main argument now would be in behalf of the player. I would make for him the same request that I would make for any other laboring man, that he be allowed one day in seven to call his own." Although other teams sometimes scheduled Sunday double-headers against the Giants to avoid facing him, Mathewson never did pitch on a Sunday.

He was frequently referred to as "the Christian gentleman," and this was another aspect of his character that enhanced his public appeal. Regardless of whether they agreed with his decision not to play on Sundays, people respected him for standing up for his religious principles. He showed that there was more to life than playing ball, and he was admired for it.

Mathewson's endorsements of personal virtue were primarily made in magazine articles he wrote and in his novels for boys. Although his baseball stories contained underlying themes about sportsmanship and values, his message was not explicitly religious. He left that to other players, the most famous of whom was Billy Sunday.

He was called "the fastest man in baseball." Accepting all challenges, he would run a 100-yard dash barefoot and easily defeat the swiftest player from any other team. Fans, players, and even team owners bet heavily on these races.

He displayed his speed only occasionally in actual games because he didn't get on base all that often. He struck out in each of his first thirteen big league at bats and never amounted to much as a hitter. But when he did get on, he was soon streaking down the base path and hook-sliding his way to another stolen base. The player-manager of the Chicago White Stockings, Cap Anson, said his young teammate "could run the bases like a frightened deer." To the fans' delight, he would run more often than not when he had the chance. By way of comparison, Ty Cobb, during his best stolen base year, had 96 steals while collecting 208 hits and 118 walks. Sunday stole 71 bases during a season in which he had only 119 hits and 12 walks.

He was also impressive as a fielder. One sportswriter said that no outfielder before him "ever covered more ground or showed such uncanny judgment as to where fly balls would light. Sunday was the ballhawk of his day."

A farm boy from Iowa, William Ashley Sunday had joined a rough and ribald crew. The White Stockings players excelled on the field and enjoyed life off it. They were frequent patrons of Chicago's downtown bars, and they took young Billy with them. One night in 1886, Sunday and several teammates had just emerged from a saloon when they encountered, at the corner of Van Buren and State Streets, a gospel wagon—a horse-drawn outpost of an evangelistic rescue mission—complete with preacher, brass band, and hymn singers. Sunday listened to a few hymns, then turned to his teammates and said, "Boys, I bid the old life goodbye." He followed the wagon back to the mission.

He kept playing ball, but spent his spare time at the Pacific Garden Mission and a Chicago YMCA, where he began his evangelistic preaching. His celebrity as a ballplayer drew curious crowds, and his natural skill as a speaker kept them attentive.

He often spoke about how prayer helped him as a ballplayer. In his preaching, he cited a game when, in the ninth inning, he was chasing a long outfield fly that carried into an area where benches had been placed for spectators.

"The crowd opened up like the Red Sea did for the rod of Moses, and as I ran and leaped those benches I said one of the swiftest prayers that was ever offered. It was, 'Lord, if ever you helped a mortal man, help me get that ball.'"

"Tell it, Billy!"

"I went over the benches as though wings were carrying me up. I threw out my hand while in the air and the ball struck and stuck. The game was ours."

"Praise the Lord!"

"Though the deduction is hardly orthodox, I am sure the Lord helped me catch that ball, and it was my first great lesson in prayer."

"Amen, Billy!"

Sunday was traded from Chicago to Pittsburgh in 1888. A Pittsburgh newspaper welcomed "the famous sprinter with the sabbatical name," and the team president praised Sunday's off-field activities, saying, "I wish we had more ballplayers like that young man."

Despite his popularity, he was traded from Pittsburgh to Philadelphia in 1890, and he signed a lucrative three-year contract. But he felt the tug of his other career, and asked the Philadelphia team to release him so he could work full-time as an evangelist. After initially refusing, the team let him go. The Cincinnati ball club immediately offered him an even better deal, but he and his wife agreed that he had been called, so he accepted a job with the YMCA for $83 a month, rather than playing for Cincinnati for $500 a month.

Sunday soon began traveling through small Midwest farm communities, like the one where he had grown up, preaching to those intrigued by "the baseball evangelist." In some towns, residents came together to build a tabernacle where he could hold his revivals. When the day's construction work was done, he would put on his major league uniform and play ball with the locals.

After years of preaching in small and midsize towns, Sunday finally broke through, with long stays in big cities as his popularity grew. During his career, which lasted into the 1930s, he was estimated to have preached to 100 million people and to have shaken the hands of a million of them. His fame reached beyond his followers, and he became a national celebrity. He was happy to engage in publicity stunts such as leading a team of evangelists in a baseball game against a team of Hollywood stars captained by Douglas Fairbanks. When the evangelists lost, Sunday jokingly remarked that it was because they couldn't get a break from the umpires, Charlie Chaplin and Mary Pickford.

Sunday was not shy about using the power that accompanied his fame. In Atlanta, in 1917, he insisted on preaching to African-Americans, and he once brought a large black choir to sing before a white audience. He also campaigned persistently for Prohibition, delivering his anti-alcohol "Get on the Water Wagon" sermon time and again.

Throughout his career, he told stories about his days in baseball. He even displayed his athleticism during his revivals, sliding across the stage like a ballplayer sliding across home plate. In a magazine article, he wrote: "Baseball is American to the core. What other sport could so characteristically serve as the play outlet for the nervous, high-strung, third-rail, double-barreled, greased-lightning, strenuous, hustling, bustling bunch of folks—bless 'em!—that inhabit this country today?"

Not all evangelists were so well-disposed toward baseball. Preacher Sam Jones said, "There is not a more corrupting thing this side of Hell than baseball," because it diverted people from more worthwhile pursuits.

Sunday, however, said that baseball was "a pure, clean, wholesome game, and there is no disgrace to any man today for playing professional baseball." He used the sport to illustrate strengths of American character. He spoke of bases stolen and catches made, and about athletes who could be shining examples during a time of spiritual regeneration. Sunday thought America needed "a tidal wave of religion, a cyclone of redemption," and he believed that sports heroes could help enlist a larger public in this revival of the spirit.

Mathewson was the kind of player Sunday cited as a paragon: accomplished as an athlete, steadfast in personal morality, an exemplar of Christian faith. The attributes Sunday touted were a good match with Mathewson's public and private persona. Such characteristics were also being referred to more frequently as national, as well as personal, virtues. Reflecting their country's growing maturity, Americans were inclined to view the United States as a moral, as well as powerful, nation.

That meshed well with Mathewson's image and with the continuing evolution of baseball. The rowdy reputation of the game was increasingly consigned to the past, and the sport and its players became more "establishment" in demeanor and appeal. The symbolism of baseball as a national institution was also taking hold. Baseball pioneer A. G. Spalding talked in 1910 about the continuing expansion of the game's constituency: "The boys of the past generation are the spectators of this; the boys of this one will be the spectators of the next. So, like an endless chain, baseball will last and grow as long as these United States shall last and grow. Each generation will produce a little higher type of citizenship than that which went before it, and baseball and the principles which underlie it will help to bring this about."

Spalding's lofty sentiments reflected baseball executives' desire to strengthen the perceived connection between baseball and nation. Doing so was in the game's interest, and the success of this linkage continues to this day. Although baseball's popularity has been challenged by other sports, it is still the game most associated with the trappings of the American spirit. The tradition of the Fourth of July picnic, with hot dogs, fireworks, and baseball is partly real, partly imagined, but certainly widely embraced. It was during Mathewson's time that the professional game became established as part of baseball's symbolic status.

After winning three straight pennants and losing three straight World Series, the Giants had acquired the reputation of being a regular season powerhouse, but a flawed team under pressure. This failure frustrated Mathewson, and he wrote a long article about it for *Everybody's Magazine* in 1914. Titled "Why We Lost Three World's Championships," the piece identified a consistent postseason problem for the team: "The Giants blew up." Mathewson wrote: "Almost without exception, every man on our team fell below his standard. Self-consciousness, overanxiety, and nervousness weighed on our shoulders."

The root cause of this, Mathewson suggested, was that most of the players had become overly dependent on manager John McGraw. "We have won the last three National League pennants," he wrote,

The Factoryville, Pennsylvania town band, circa 1894. Mathewson is second row, second from left. (National Baseball Hall of Fame Library, Cooperstown, New York)

Teacher and student. Manager John McGraw and Mathewson. (National Baseball Hall of Fame Library, Cooperstown, New York)

*The matinee idol.
Mathewson soon after
joining the Giants.
(National Baseball
Hall of Fame Library,
Cooperstown, New York)*

Fans at New York's Polo Grounds, 1911. (Library of Congress)

The baseball-loving president, William Howard Taft, with Washington's Clark Griffith, 1912. (National Baseball Hall of Fame Library, Cooperstown, New York)

Giants pitcher Rube Marquard with his wife, vaudeville star Blossom Seeley. (National Baseball Hall of Fame Library, Cooperstown, New York)

Billy Sunday, "the fastest man in baseball," who became one of the nation's best known evangelists. (National Baseball Hall of Fame Library, Cooperstown, New York)

Jane, Christy Jr., and Christy, circa 1912. (National Baseball Hall of Fame Library, Cooperstown, New York)

The icon: a portrait of Mathewson on the cover of Baseball Magazine, *1914. (National Baseball Hall of Fame Library, Cooperstown, New York)*

Woodrow Wilson, another president who was a devoted fan, at Opening Day 1916. (National Baseball Hall of Fame Library, Cooperstown, New York)

Mathewson as manager of the Cincinnati Reds. (National Baseball Hall of Fame Library, Cooperstown, New York)

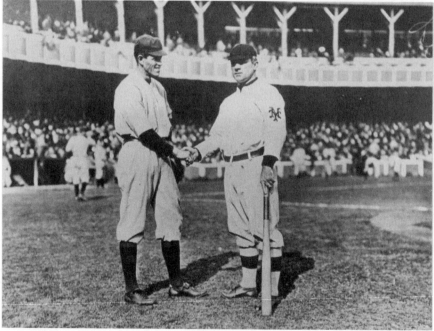

Baseball's biggest scoundrel, Hal Chase (l.), here with his sometime protector, John McGraw. (National Baseball Hall of Fame Library, Cooperstown, New York)

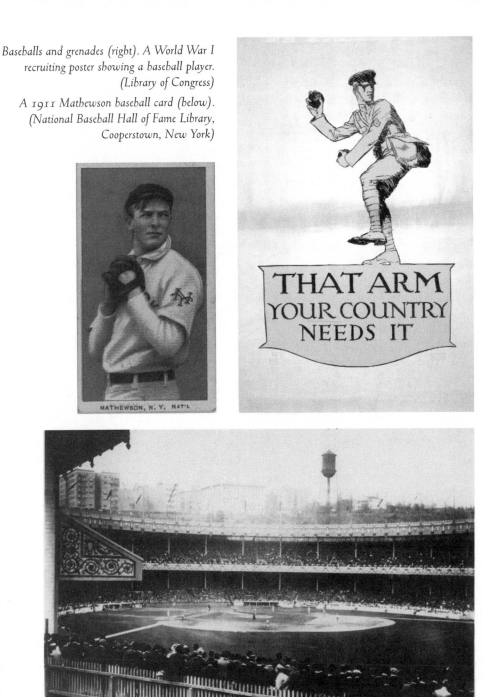

Baseballs and grenades (right). A World War I recruiting poster showing a baseball player. (Library of Congress)

A 1911 Mathewson baseball card (below). (National Baseball Hall of Fame Library, Cooperstown, New York)

THAT ARM
YOUR COUNTRY
NEEDS IT

MATHEWSON, N. Y. NAT'L

The Polo Grounds during the 1913 World Series, which the Giants lost to the Philadelphia Athletics. (Library of Congress)

Captain Mathewson,
Chemical Warfare
Service, U.S. Army.
(National Baseball Hall
of Fame Library,
Cooperstown, New York)

Mathewson selling Christmas
Seals to New York Mayor John
F. Hylan, December 1922.
(National Baseball Hall of
Fame Library, Cooperstown,
New York)

"solely because the club is McGraw, because his baseball brains have directed every game. . . . " Mathewson made clear that he was not criticizing McGraw. But, he added, "stricken with a case of nerves, the system went to pieces. The Giants did not obey orders. They either forgot or convinced themselves that they knew more than the wonderful little manager who had guided them so long." In the final game of the 1911 Series, he said, "growing more and more nervous and self-conscious under the tension, we snapped in a way that made us look ridiculous."

Although the 1912 World Series was the most excruciating failure for the Giants, the defeat further defined Mathewson as a model of classy sportsmanship. In the second game of the Series, five Giant errors led to four unearned Boston runs, and Mathewson, who pitched eleven innings, saw the game end in a 6-6 tie when it was called because of darkness. In his next start, Mathewson gave up just five hits and one earned run, but a Giant error let in another run. After that, Matty retired the next 17 batters, but the Giants still lost 2-1.

The most heartbreaking game was the final one. After trailing in the Series three games to one, the Giants had fought back to tie it at three games each. After nine innings of the seventh game, the score was 2-2. The Giants pushed across a run in the top of the tenth and were poised to win the championship.

Back in New York, thousands of Giants fans watched a huge "bulletin board" outside the *New York American*'s offices at Broadway and Park Place that detailed every play. Throughout the game, as Mathewson extricated himself from tight spots, the downtown streets echoed with cheers. In the tenth, the cheers became a roar when the Giants pulled ahead. And then—disaster.

The first Red Sox batter, Clyde Engle, sent an easy fly to center field. The Giants' Fred Snodgrass circled under it, put up his glove . . . and dropped the ball. Engle ended up on second. Snodgrass partly redeemed himself on the next play, making a running catch of a line drive. Mathewson then walked Steve Yerkes. The next batter, Tris Speaker, popped up a foul near first base. Mathewson, catcher Chief Meyers, and first baseman Fred Merkle converged on it, but they all froze and the ball dropped between them. As he headed back to the batter's box, Speaker told Mathewson, "Matty, that play will cost you the game and the Series." He then knocked a single to right, scoring Engle with the tying run. McGraw, hoping to set up a double play at any base, ordered Matty to walk the next batter. With the bases loaded, Boston third baseman Larry Gardner hit a long fly to right, and Yerkes scored the winning run after the catch.

Sportswriter Fred Lieb said, "In my many years of following the World Series, I never saw such dejection as that of the New York contingent. . . . The Giants just missed winning it by an eyelash—really two eyelashes," the two inexplicable muffs. He wrote that his colleague Sid Mercer of the *New York Globe* had tears rolling down his cheeks as he dictated details to his paper's telegrapher.

Mathewson, meanwhile, walked off the mound and, to an ovation from the Boston fans, congratulated Red Sox pitcher Smoky Joe Wood. He then consoled Snodgrass in the Giants' clubhouse, and on the train back to New York tried to bolster his teammates' spirits. Despite the fielding lapses behind him throughout the Series, he had no harsh words for anyone. He said of Snodgrass, "No use hopping on him; he feels three times as bad as any of us."

Boston mayor John "Honey Fitz" Fitzgerald (grandfather of John F. Kennedy) praised his hometown Red Sox but said that Matty was the hero of the Series. A New York editorial said of Mathewson, "In victory he was admirable, but in defeat he was magnificent."

By this time Mathewson had become a tribal elder among the Giants. He was the only player left on the team who had been a member of the World Champion Giants of 1905. He remained very close personally to McGraw, who counted on his star pitcher to maintain high standards on and off the field and to serve as a role model for younger players.

McGraw was constantly trying to figure out ways to strengthen and energize his team, and not just by picking up new players. One of his ideas was to move spring training to a remote site where players would not be distracted by saloons, racetracks, or pool halls. He settled on Marlin, Texas, a small town about 160 miles south of Dallas.

The Giants lived at Marlin's Arlington Hotel, which lacked niceties such as private bathrooms, and trained at the town's ballpark, which had been renovated, after a fashion, and deeded to the Giants for as long as they chose to stay. The Texans made the Giants feel welcome, holding fish fries for them on the Brazos River and hosting dances to honor their visitors. McGraw, to reciprocate, ended the team's stay each spring with a dinner dance for the residents of Marlin.

The players would walk the mile from their hotel to the ballpark and work hard in the Texas heat, concentrating on fundamentals such as the hook slide, which McGraw considered an essential tool of the game. Mathewson tutored some of the younger players on technique, and he also adopted some of McGraw's gruffness. When a rookie asked him, "Do you think Honus Wagner is as good as Ty Cobb?" Mathewson responded, "Did you come down here to learn to play ball or with the idea that you are attending some sort of conversational soiree?"

McGraw did his best to keep his players focused solely on baseball during spring training. Some, however, such as Rube Marquard, couldn't stay out of trouble. The young pitcher decided that since he was in Texas, he ought to have a six-shooter. And once he got it, he might as well use it. He practiced his marksmanship on the lights of the local movie theater's marquee. Only McGraw's fistful of dollars kept Marquard out of the town jail.

Mathewson was well behaved, of course, but he wistfully recalled that "when I was a young fellow and read about the big league clubs going South, I used to think what a grand life that must be. Riding in Pullmans, some pleasant exercise which did not entail the responsibility of a ball game, and plenty of food, with a little social recreation, were all parts of my dream." Reality, he added, was different: "My idea of no setting for a pleasure party is Marlin Springs, Texas." His "social recreation" consisted primarily of playing checkers in the lobby of the Arlington, which always drew a crowd of spectators, including Jane, who dutifully endured the small town isolation with her husband.

Nevertheless, Mathewson was not averse to spending more time in Texas if the money was right. One autumn, after the Giants schedule had been completed, he joined the El Paso White Sox for the final three weeks of their late-running season. This was common practice for big league stars. That same autumn Rube Waddell pitched for the Socorro, New Mexico, team, and other players were scattered through the Southwest. The *El Paso Herald* said of Mathewson's impending arrival, "This is about the best single piece of baseball news that has broke into this burg since it was decided to make the El Paso team a professional one."

Noting that Mathewson's presence would give El Paso the opportunity to upgrade its image, the newspaper inveighed against the sale of beer in the grandstand during games. Beer sales, the paper said, "will create an impression of rowdyism in the minds of our visitors, which is the very thing El Paso has been trying to live down since the exit of the gamblers and their ruffian crew."

El Paso wasn't the only place where a beverage debate raged. Even Congress became involved, passing a bill that required the ballpark in Washington, D.C., to offer fans free drinking water in paper cups. The bill was sponsored by a Georgia congressman who resented having to pay ten cents a bottle for sarsaparilla. Some fans opposed the measure, fearing that the sarsaparilla salesmen and their bottled goods would be driven out of business. The fans needed those bottles. One said, "What's the use of trying to bean an umpire with a paper cup?"

While such issues were being debated in American ballparks, the Giants occasionally made their way to more exotic locales such as Havana, where Mathewson indulged his fondness for Cuban food and, as always, for checkers. He became renowned in Havana for taking on six opponents simultaneously and beating them all.

Touring American teams often lost most of their games against the Cuban ball clubs, many of which included black American players who were kept out of the major leagues. During their 1911 visit, however, the Giants did well against their Cuban opponents; the high point was a pitching duel in which Mathewson, throwing a three-hitter, bested Cuban ace Jose Mendez.

Although his status as popular hero was undiminished, Mathewson's pitching career was nearing its end. He went 24-13 in 1914, which was to be his last winning season.

His arm was tired and sore, there was no doubt about that. But he still knew how to pitch and had his excellent control. Ring Lardner wrote: "They ain't nobody else in the world that can stick a ball as near where they want to stick it as he can. I bet he could shave you if he wanted to and if he had a razor blade to throw instead of a ball. If you can't hit a fast one a inch and a quarter inside and he knows it, you'll get three fast ones a inch and a quarter inside." Sportswriter F. C. Lane echoed this, observing, "To Mathewson more than to any other pitcher of his time, or of any other time, was given the gift of placing a baseball exactly where he wanted it."

Mathewson pitched 4,782 regular season innings during his career and walked 846 batters. That works out to 1.6 walks per nine innings. During four World Series, he pitched 102 innings and walked only 10, less than one per game. He struck out 2,502 regular season batters during his career, an average just under five strikeouts per nine innings. This was a substantial number at the time. Even Walter Johnson averaged only slightly more than five strikeouts every nine innings. Mathewson threw pitches that could be hit, but not very hard, and relied on his defense. This meant that games went quickly. In one of his complete games, he threw only 67 pitches.

In his first appearance of the 1915 season, his arm wouldn't obey him. His curve had lost its bite and his fastball had no zip. He quickly gave up four runs and lasted only three innings. Other poor performances followed, and Mathewson finished the year 8-14, his first losing season—and the first season in which he had not won at least 22 games—since 1902. The Giants, who had finished second in 1914, plunged into last place.

McGraw could fix the team, but Mathewson could not restore his arm. After appearing in 647 games—445 of which were complete games—Mathewson was simply pitched out. And so what once would have been unthinkable happened. Midway into the 1916 season, after Mathewson had appeared in just 12 games with a 3-4 record, the Giants traded him.

This was not as cold-blooded as it may sound. McGraw knew that Mathewson wanted to be a manager, so he arranged a deal with the Cincinnati Reds that brought Cincinnati's player-manager Buck Herzog, along with Red Killefer, to New York in exchange for Mathewson, Edd Roush, and Bill McKechnie. McGraw tried to insert a condition in the deal that would allow the Giants to get Mathewson back after two years. Presumably, if McGraw decided to retire then, Mathewson would be named manager of the Giants. But Cincinnati would not agree, and McGraw ended up managing until 1932.

Mathewson had mixed feelings about leaving. On the day of the trade he told reporters, "Why, it's all right; it's a step upward, you know." He admitted that he did not expect to pitch again, saying that he had warmed up the day before, "but this morning the same old pain was there," and trying to throw was "just like opening up a fresh wound and never giving it any chance to heal." He later told Roush: "Of course, I realize I'm through as a pitcher. But I appreciate McGraw making a place for me in baseball and getting me this managing job. He's doing me a favor, and I thanked him for it."

News reports noted that Mathewson getting a manager's job was the only way "New York fans would countenance his going." The news coverage reflected the bittersweet feeling: "While New York is sorry to lose Matty, who has long been dear to the hearts of fans not only here but throughout the country, it is glad to see him graduate to a leadership. He will make good. Matty could never fail in baseball, no matter what his undertaking."

The Cincinnati press applauded the Reds' move. Mathewson, said the *Cincinnati Enquirer*, had been McGraw's adviser and "is a deep student of the pastime. There is no doubt that he will command the respect of the players and will get the best work out of the team. As a coach and judge of pitchers, he is in a class by himself."

With a few exceptions, the Cincinnati team was weak, particularly its pitching staff. Of the 68 games in 1916 with Mathewson as their manager, the Reds won only 25. Mathewson knew he needed to rebuild the team, much as McGraw had rebuilt the Giants when he first arrived in New York.

He welcomed the challenge and plunged right in, searching the minor leagues for new players. In one telegram to Reds owner Garry Herrmann, Mathewson listed prospects worth acquiring from teams in Utica, Portland, Reading, Moline, and Tulsa.

The contract with Cincinnati specified that Mathewson was to be "player and manager," but it included a clause granting Mathewson the right "to exercise his own discretion as to when he shall play ball during the term of this contract." Mathewson pitched just once for Cincinnati, against his old rival Three Finger Brown, who was about to retire and was pitching his final game for Chicago. Over the years, the two had faced each other 24 times, with each winning 12 of the games. This final encounter was evidence that both pitchers were finished. Mathewson and the Reds won, 10-8, but he gave up 15 hits while Brown gave up 19.

The *Cincinnati Enquirer* reported: "In spite of the brutal manner in which the two veterans were treated by the opposing batters, it was an inspiring sight to see them matched once more. . . . Neither man was the pitcher of old. Their stuff was gone, their speed was lacking, their curves were conspicuous by their absence. But both were still there with the brains and the courage of yore, with the spirit that would never acknowledge defeat and with the undying nerve of the true artist. Their work was a lesson to the young pitchers who sat on the benches and gazed at the old masters."

It was Mathewson's 373rd regular season victory, and it marked the end of his career as a player. He had just turned thirty-six.

It did not, however, mean the end of his influence on baseball. As a manager and later as a team executive, Mathewson would remain a resolute proponent of high standards of play and sportsmanship. His commitment to the moral dimensions of sport would extend into broader issues of citizenship.

Mathewson's interests reflected a renewal of idealism in American life, as exemplified by the former college professor now residing in the White House.

Thomas Woodrow Wilson was a lifelong baseball fan. Before he began using his middle name, when he left college, he was Tommy Wilson—just another kid who loved to play the game. In his notebook from Davidson College, which he attended for a year before transferring to Princeton, is his elegantly handwritten list of the "Nines of Davidson College." On the "Fresh Nine 1873–74," at second base, is "T. W. Wilson."

At Princeton, he remained devoted to baseball. In one diary entry he laments, "This is the first day this week that I have not played baseball." But the next day was more typical: "Read a little oratory this morning. . . . Very interesting work. Played the Lit boys at noon five innings and beat them by a score of 8 to 7. . . . I pitched."

He also attended games as a spectator. In June 1876, after spending the morning in a Latin exam, he watched a game between Princeton and a professional team. Princeton lost, he wrote, but "our fellows played beautifully. . . . It was the best game I ever saw." On another day: "Was called upon to recite in Greek testament and in Demosthenes. Worked on my essay at odd intervals during the day. At noon went to the baseball grounds to see the university nine practice." In the spring of 1877, Wilson wrote that losses to Yale and Harvard had thrown him "into a state of despondency."

Wilson was editor of the campus newspaper, the *Princetonian*, and he wrote many of its news stories, including accounts of baseball games. He and the paper lobbied for tighter organization of Princeton's sports teams, especially baseball, and called for regular practices, improved coaching, and better discipline. In 1878, Wilson was elected president of the baseball team (something like being general manager), but he later resigned—after consulting with his mother—in order to have time for a heavier academic load.

When Wilson returned to Princeton in 1890 as a faculty member, he was still a devoted fan of baseball and other sports. He was known to cheer the university teams with unprofessorial ardor, as if he was still an undergraduate. Once while he was traveling abroad, his wife wrote him with news of Princeton's victory over Yale in the third and deciding game of their annual series, which was played at New York's Polo Grounds.

His affection for baseball never faltered. As president, he continued Taft's practice of throwing out the first ball on opening day. His presence at a game was considered a good luck charm by Washington players, who almost always won when he was in the stands. In 1917, the season began a few days after the United States declared war on

Germany, so Wilson assigned the opening day toss to Vice President Thomas Marshall, also a longtime fan. In a pregame ceremony, an extra-large American flag was hoisted on the outfield flagpole by a delegation led by Assistant Secretary of the Navy Franklin D. Roosevelt.

Even in his postpresidential years, when his health was poor, Wilson made his way to Washington's ballpark to watch Walter Johnson and his teammates.

Despite his long history as participant and fan, Wilson was not perceived as being an athlete in the Theodore Roosevelt mold. Of course Roosevelt assiduously promoted that image, while Wilson didn't care. Nevertheless, there was an important connection between Wilson and athletics, and the moral standards Wilson endorsed were closely related to the values of sportsmanship reflected by Mathewson.

In 1895, the thirty-eight-year-old professor wrote to his wife: "That I am an idealist, with the heart of a poet, I do not hesitate to avow, but that fact is not reassuring. On the contrary, it is tragical." Wilson understood that idealists are likely to find their goals beyond their grasp. Despite their noble efforts, they inevitably fall short and end up with their hearts broken.

But for a while, he was able to wield his idealism as a politically potent weapon. As the Democratic nominee for governor of New Jersey in 1910, he criticized President Taft, saying, "The American people are disappointed because he has not led them," and he offered his own high-toned summons to an idealized politics. "We are witnessing a renaissance of public spirit," he said, "a reawakening of sober public opinion, a revival of the power of the people, the beginning of an age of thoughtful reconstruction that makes our thought hark back to the great age in which democracy was set up in America." He also told voters that Americans were on the threshold of "the age in which politics is a great altruistic undertaking."

Wilson won the governorship and rose quickly. Less than three years later he delivered his first inaugural address as president, prom-ising "to cleanse, to reconsider, to restore . . . to lift everything that concerns our life as a nation to the light that shines from the heart-fire of every man's conscience and vision of the right."

In his speeches, Wilson tried to define himself and his politics. He believed that the institutions and practices of American politics were being corrupted by expedience and could be redeemed only by a restoration of principle. This was the idealist in power, convinced that his cause would triumph.

His mandate, however, was less than solid. Although he won an electoral vote landslide in the three-way race (receiving 435 electoral votes to Roosevelt's 88 and Taft's 6), he was a minority president in terms of the popular vote, receiving 45 percent of the 14 million votes cast. The vote can be looked at in two ways: that the two "Republicans" in the race—GOP nominee Taft and breakaway Bull Moose candidate Roosevelt—received 55 percent of the votes; or that the two "reform" candidates—Wilson and Roosevelt—between them garnered 75 percent of the vote. Wilson, of course, preferred the latter interpretation, although he remained sensitive to the per-ception "that I represent a minority of the nation."

This concern did not diminish his belief in his mission, and he added an ample dose of moralism to his speeches. Historians have noted the religious foundation of Wilson's view of moral duty. John Morton Blum wrote, "His basic, lifelong faith was in the individual as a distinct moral agent, inspired by and accountable to God." John Milton Cooper observed that Wilson "resembled other American Protestants in holding strong views about personal and social moral-ity, and he believed that life was a serious business, to be lived accord-ing to God's purposes. But he always remained humble about presuming to know what those purposes were."

Wilson's religious views informed his approach to the presidency. Historian Eric Goldman wrote, "If under Roosevelt social reform had taken on all the excitement of a circus, under Wilson it acquired the dedication of a sunrise service."

It was in foreign policy that Wilson most clearly articulated his vision of America, first in a determined effort to keep the United States out of war, and then to ensure that America led its allies to a victory of ideals as well as arms. "The force of America," he said, "is the force of moral principle." Moral authority, he argued, had its own exceptional power. In 1915, several days after the *Lusitania* was sunk by a German submarine, Wilson said: "The example of America must be a special example. . . . There is such a thing as a man being too proud to fight. There is such a thing as a nation being so right that it does not need to convince others by force that it is right."

The phrase "a nation being so right" reflected Wilson's sense of national rectitude—a loftiness ensuring that America would be the "special example" of which he spoke. Seeking to elevate the expectations Americans had for themselves, he linked standards for individual citizens to those for nations. In 1916, in his first comments about a prospective "league of peace," he said, "It is clear that nations must in the future be governed by the same high code of honor that we demand of individuals."

Pledged to keeping America out of war, but acknowledging the need for preparedness, Wilson portrayed the United States—this young, emerging world power—as standing above the traditional behavior of competing nations. "We are, indeed," he said, "a true friend to all the nations of the world, because we threaten none, covet the possessions of none, desire the overthrow of none. Our friendship can be accepted and is accepted without reservation, because it is offered in a spirit and for a purpose which no one need ever question or suspect. Therein lies our greatness."

The ingenuousness in such pronouncements can be viewed as admirable or self-defeating. Wilson's critics, such as Theodore Roosevelt, considered idealism that was not reinforced by pragmatism to be of little value. But many Americans responded, at least for a while, to Wilson's appeals to an innate nobility that was presumed to be part of a distinctly American character.

In April 1917, when Wilson finally had to ask Congress for a declaration of war, he maintained the virtuous outlook. "Our motive," he said, "will not be revenge or the victorious assertion of the physical might of the nation, but only the vindication of right, of human right, of which we are only a single champion."

Two years later, with the war ended, Wilson again stressed America's special moral responsibility. "America," he said, "is the hope of the world. And if she does not justify that hope, results are unthinkable." As he stumped the country to win support for the peace treaty, he returned again and again to the theme of America's duty: "America is necessary to the peace of the world."

On his ill-fated whistle-stop tour in 1919, during which he suffered the stroke that effectively ended his presidency, Wilson spoke of how he saw himself and his country: "Sometimes people call me an idealist. Well, that is the way I know I am an American. . . . America is the only idealistic nation in the world." Some Wilson critics have argued that his clinging to idealism is evidence of his naivete. But as historian Philip Bobbitt notes, the man who "skillfully took his country from stubborn isolationism to world leadership is unlikely to have based his decisions on a childlike view of human nature."

Wilson's persistent idealism legitimized the views of others who embraced a high-minded approach to personal standards. Historian John Morton Blum observed, "Like Wilson, most Americans preferred their issues moral, their honor pure, their peace preserved."

Twenty years earlier, professional sports and idealism would not have been a good match. Mathewson would have been a lonely champion of sportsmanship and of the compatibility of baseball and personal virtue. But in Woodrow Wilson's America, principle mattered, and Mathewson was in the mainstream. Wilson's pledge "to cleanse, to reconsider, to restore" and his insistence on a "high code of honor" found an acolyte in Mathewson, who set his own work ethic and personal code on the highest plane.

He was soon to demonstrate that, more assertively than ever before, in baseball and beyond.

SIX

Elevating the Game

WILSON HAD CRITICS who found him more preachy than wise, and so did Mathewson. Although most of his teammates admired Mathewson, a few thought that this ballplayer who brought a Bible with him on road trips and presumed to define proper behavior was insufferable. "He was a pinhead," said outfielder Jack Hendricks. "He didn't care about anybody except himself." Hendricks also said that some players found Mathewson so stuck-up that they stopped speaking to him, and that several put forth less than their best effort in the field behind him. (It should be noted that Hendricks played in only eight games for the Giants.)

When Mathewson went to Cincinnati as manager, his contract gave him the authority to enforce his own standards. One clause allowed him "to discipline by fine, suspension or otherwise, any player of the club as he . . . may deem advisable."

He did not hesitate to take charge and make judgments. As he prepared for the 1917 season, he sent a series of letters to team owner Garry Herrmann, indicating what kinds of players he wanted and didn't want. He shied away from one trade because the player who was to be acquired "has been in and out of 'fast company.'" He also asked Herrmann about signing catcher Larry McLean, who, said Mathewson, "wants to reform." Mathewson went on to say: "I had a long talk with him two days ago. I asked him how he expected to get in shape. He said: 'If you sign me, I will start to train right now, and won't take a drink during the season. Furthermore, I would want everybody in America to know that I was on the water wagon.'" Mathewson added that McLean had been "easy to manage when not drinking." But, Mathewson warned, "If he drinks, he is not worth keeping on a ball club." Mathewson told Herrmann he could sign McLean for a low salary but then equivocated, saying, "I am neutral." Herrmann took that as a negative signal from his manager, and McLean did not play in the big leagues again.

Mathewson was wise to the ways of players who wanted to juice up the contracts they had been offered. When pitcher Fred Toney (who proved to be the ace of Mathewson's 1917 staff) held out for more money, Mathewson told Herrmann: "I am of the opinion that he will sign his contract after writing a few more letters, and I do not think that I could hurry him by writing him. Of course, we will not consider letting him go to another club."

Mathewson seemed comfortable in his new role. He avoided the frustration that plagues some superstars-turned-managers by recognizing that not every player would reach the level he himself had performed at. He possessed a sophisticated understanding of the strategies, tactics, and rhythms of the game. His own intelligence, refined by years of McGraw's tutelage, made him a well-equipped manager. The Cincinnati team got better, and Mathewson's leadership was clearly a major factor in that change.

Instilling his standards for sportsmanship and personal conduct proved a greater challenge. Before long, his refusal to ignore player misbehavior would lead him into the fiercest controversy of his career.

In the meantime, baseball fit nicely into the peaceful haven that America had carved out for itself. As the Great War raged in Europe, President Wilson found isolationism to be politically and morally convenient, and America attended to more mundane matters. The Navy Department ended the serving of alcohol on its vessels, and a number of laws paving the way to Prohibition were upheld in court. The General Federation of Women's Clubs urged that the tango be banned. Transcontinental telephone service began, with Alexander Graham Bell duplicating his 1876 call to Thomas Watson: "Mr. Watson, come here, I want you." This time, however, the two men were not in adjoining rooms; Bell was in New York and Watson was in San Francisco.

The tenuous state of American innocence was reflected in the work of one of the country's most popular novelists, Booth Tarkington. The years just before America entered the war were among his most successful in a long career that attracted millions of readers. Three of his books in that period were bestsellers: in 1914, *Penrod* ranked seventh on the year's list; in 1915, *The Turmoil* was number one; and in 1916, *Seventeen* was also number one.

Penrod and *Seventeen* are funny, charming books about growing up in an environment largely untouched by concerns of the larger world. Like Mark Twain's *Tom Sawyer*, these books are about young people but they were not written especially for young readers. They allow adults to recapture a bit of their own childhoods. Tarkington reminds his readers that "maturity forgets the marvelous realness of a boy's day-dreams, how colorful they glow, rosy and living, and how opaque the curtain closing down between the dreamer and the actual world."

Penrod Schofield is twelve years old and has elevated mischief-making to an art form. He is a descendant of Twain's boys, a character both realistic and fanciful. So, too, is seventeen-year-old Willie Baxter, the hero of *Seventeen*. This book tells the story of Willie's summer, spent "mooning along" in the wake of a teenage femme fatale, the blonde, baby-talking Lola Pratt. Willie must also endure endless torture inflicted by his ten-year-old sister and the frustrating calmness of his parents. Willie's is a chaste courtship, marked by his comic missteps and Lola's saccharine obnoxiousness. The milieu in which they perform their social minuet is that of solid, upper-middle-class normalcy. Willie, Lola, and a bevy of friends picnic at a nearby farm and dance through a summer night in a neighborhood backyard. There are afternoon teas and conversations on moonlit front porches. As with America itself, in *Penrod* and *Seventeen* the outside world is kept a comfortable distance away.

The Turmoil, which Tarkington wrote between the two "boys' novels," is very different. It owes more to Dickens than to Twain, and is set in "a dirty and wonderful city nesting dingily in the fog of its own smoke," where wealth is "better loved than cleanliness." The voice of this city is hoarse, hot, and rapacious, with one refrain: "Wealth! I will get Wealth! I will make Wealth! I will sell Wealth for more Wealth! My house shall be dirty, my garment shall be dirty, and I will foul my neighbor so that he cannot be clean—but I will get Wealth!"

There would be no room for Penrod or Willie in this city. Their innocence would be smothered by the cynicism here. As for the voice of the people, "The politicians let the people make all the laws they liked; it did not matter much. . . . They made laws for all things and forgot them immediately; though sometimes they would remember after a while, and hurry to make new laws that the old laws should be enforced—and then forget both new and old. Wherever enforcement threatened Money or Votes—or wherever it was too much bother—it became a joke. Influence was the law."

That doesn't sound like the way things were supposed to work in Woodrow Wilson's progressive democracy. Tarkington didn't think so, either. He wanted to raise the alarm about the unrestrained materialism and unprincipled business practices that he believed were ruining American life. The city in *The Turmoil* was modeled on Indianapolis, which as described in the book bore little resemblance to the Indianapolis where Tarkington had been born in 1869. He remembered his Indiana boyhood and reminded his readers that there were alternatives to industrial dominance of the environment. In *The Turmoil*, he describes a drive in the country past fields and sun-flecked groves of trees, where it was possible to "breathe the rushing clean air beneath a glorious sky—that sky so despised in the city, and so maltreated there, that . . . it was impossible for men to remember that blue is the rightful color overhead." Also in the city, trees were dying, and "Bigness" replaced them with telephone and electric light poles. "They were hideous, but nobody minded that; and sometimes the wires fell and killed people—but not often enough to matter."

Tarkington believed that not just the air and land were being mistreated. As he illustrated with the stories of his protagonists in *The Turmoil*, the Sheridan family, the American character was also suffering under the pressures of unchecked greed.

All this was part of a larger historical shift that was testing Wilson's presidency. After just a few more years, at the end of the World War, the United States would emerge in the position it was to maintain for the rest of the century: the world's dominant economic and military power. The dichotomy between the world of *Penrod* and *Seventeen* and that of *The Turmoil* reflected the nation's political and spiritual growing pains.

Baseball could narrow that gap and ease those pains by keeping one foot on the terrain of Penrod's and Willie's sandlot innocence while putting the other in the domain of the Sheridans' commercial crassness. Then as now baseball was a business, but also more than a business. The tug-of-war between tradition and modernity, the game itself and commercialism, continues in baseball today. The economics of the sport at the major league level—astronomical players' salaries, expensive tickets, corporate values—coexist with nostalgia that is reflected in the design of many new ballparks.

During the changing times that Tarkington surveyed, popular heroes were in demand, partly as symbols of stability and continuity. They were living proof that American virtue had not been swept away by "progress." One of those heroes who had much in common with Mathewson, in terms of athletic talent and personal character, was Hobey Baker.

He would take the puck and circle behind his own goal, building up speed. Then, as he flashed down the ice, the crowd would rise and cheer, "Here he comes!"

This is what they had come to see; this is why the swells in their tuxedoes had waited in the long line of limousines to get to St. Nick's Arena. He sped past everyone else on the ice, weaving effortlessly between them, never once looking at the puck that traveled as if attached to his stick. His blond hair was a flash of gold as he reached the end of his dash and flipped the puck into the opponents' goal.

Hobart Amory Hare Baker was the quintessential amateur athlete. During his years at Princeton, he was considered the best hockey player in the world. He was also an All-American on a national champion football team and an outstanding baseball player (although he was forced to give up baseball because a university rule limited athletes to two varsity teams). In *This Side of Paradise*, F. Scott Fitzgerald used Baker as his model for Allenby, the "slim and defiant" football captain who knew "the hopes of the college rested on him, that his hundred-and-sixty pounds were expected to dodge to victory through the heavy blue and crimson lines."

Hobey Baker was admired not merely because of his athletic skills, but also because he exemplified the sportsmanship often cited as an ideal but rarely realized. After a hockey game in which he took a terrible beating from opposing players, he went to their locker room to shake their hands and tell them how much he had enjoyed the game. When one of the players apologized for banging Baker's head so hard that it knocked him out momentarily, Baker waved off the apology and said it was just part of the game. The opposing team vowed never to treat Baker so roughly again. In a football game, a Dartmouth player trying to tackle Baker was knocked cold. He later learned that Baker had carried him off the field.

It is important to remember that Baker's athletic exploits all occurred when he was in his late teens and early twenties. Despite his youth, he had a sense of moral purpose in the way he conducted himself on the ice and the gridiron. The Ivy League ruled intercollegiate sports at this time, so Baker received extensive press attention. He was a reluctant public figure, sensitive about overshadowing his teammates. He sometimes refused to go onto the ice until arena managers removed signs saying "Hobey Baker Plays Here Tonight."

Hockey has never been a genteel sport, but Baker was not a brawler. He would not retaliate if he was clobbered, no matter how unfairly, but he did defend his teammates. He was penalized only twice during his college career, and his fans argued fiercely that those calls were unfair. The Harvard hockey coach said, "He believes the rough stuff has no place in the game."

He would never take unfair advantage of an opponent. A Yale player who dumped Baker onto the ice was called for charging, but Baker protested to the referee, "He was playing the puck, not me, and that penalty could cost them the game." The referee reversed his call.

After graduating from Princeton in 1914, Baker went to work on Wall Street, but finance was no substitute for sports. He joined the St. Nicholas hockey club, a team of amateurs who paid to play and recapture the thrill of their days as college athletes. Most, like Baker, were Ivy League grads who worked as bankers or brokers. Five of his teammates had their own valets.

With war looming, Baker found a new passion—flying. He took lessons in the mornings before heading to Wall Street, and when America entered the war he was among the first U.S. pilots to go to France.

He likened a talent for aerial combat to skill as an athlete. He wrote, "You handle your machine instinctively, just as you dodge instinctively when running with the ball in an open field." When he had to pull away from an enemy plane to avoid crashing into it, he said, "It was just like missing a goal when you have gotten past the defense and have only the goal keeper to stop you."

Baker rose to become commander of a squadron (twenty-six pilots) and led them into combat until the Armistice. On the day he was supposed to leave the front for Paris, he decided to take one last flight. At six hundred feet, the Spad's engine quit. Baker tried to nurse it back to the airfield, but it plunged into the ground.

At a memorial service, Princeton president John Grier Hibben spoke of Baker's "spirit of manly vigor, of honor, of fair play, and the clean game." His hockey and football achievements remain in the record books, but like Mathewson, Baker recognized that physical accomplishment is only one aspect of sports, and that if an athlete is to be admired, it should be for making more of a contribution than scoring goals or pitching shutouts. That was a far from universally held sentiment, but the reputation of Hobey Baker will probably endure longer than those of many one-dimensional superstars.

In New York's Cathedral of St. John the Divine, one of the bays is dedicated to sports. There is a stained glass window depicting a baseball player. The names of four athletes are carved into the stone walls to acknowledge their outstanding character and sportsmanship. Two are football's Walter Camp and tennis player Robert Wrenn. The other two are Hobey Baker and Christy Mathewson.

The sports world was not wholly populated by paragons of honor. Part of the appeal of Christy Mathewson and Hobey Baker was that they were exceptional in character as well as in athletic ability. The norm was far less glorious: men who possessed considerable physical talent but who misbehaved in various ways, sometimes in the public's view, sometimes not.

The gleam of Mathewson-type moral luster might pull the public's attention away from run-of-the-mill boorishness, but occasionally an athlete's behavior was so egregious that it damaged the game he played. In baseball, no one did more harm to the sport than Hal Chase.

When Chase is spoken of today, it is usually with disdain for his misconduct. Forgotten is his enormous talent. He batted over .300 five times in his fifteen-year career, winning the 1916 National League batting title while hitting .339. He was an exceptional first baseman, and could sweep across the infield to capture a bunt and fire the ball to any base. He played far off the bag and was among the first masters of the double play that went from the first baseman to second and back to first. Score it 3-4-3 or 3-6-3. Sportswriter Fred Lieb said that as a fielder, Chase "was speed and grace personified."

But he was a crook. He bet on games, even against his own team. When he had money on the line, he would sometimes approach his own teammates, telling them they could share his winnings if they would tilt the game in the opponents' favor. More often, he would shave his own play just enough: he'd have a bit of trouble picking up a grounder; he wouldn't make it to the base in time; his throw would pull a teammate a few inches off the bag. Mixed in with his typically excellent play, the mistakes were often shrugged off by observers as just part of the game. They assumed he would make up for the slip with a great play the next inning.

Some people, however, watched him with a finer eye and a less forgiving attitude. When Chase was playing for the New York Yankees in 1913, Yankee manager Frank Chance—who had been the outstanding first baseman of the Chicago Cubs' Tinker-to-Evers-to-Chance combination—approached sportswriters Fred Lieb and Heywood Broun after a game. He said: "I want to tell you fellows what's going on. Did you notice some of the balls that got away from Chase today? They weren't wild throws; they were only made to look that way. He's been doing that right along. He's throwing games on me!"

Lieb's editor at the New York *Press* decided not to print Chance's comment. Broun, who worked for New York's *Morning Telegraph* wrote a short item for the paper noting that Chase was not performing up to his ability and was costing the Yankees some games. That earned Broun a bawling out from Yankees owner Frank Farrell, so Broun told Farrell that Frank Chance was his source. Two days later, Chase was traded to the White Sox for two so-so players.

Lieb starting watching Chase more carefully and believed that he spotted how the first baseman was cheating his team. In his memoir, Lieb wrote: "His neatest trick (I think) was to arrive at first base for a throw from another infielder just a split second too late. A third baseman, for example, must throw to the bag, whether the first baseman is there or not. Chase, playing far off the bag, probably could have got there in time, with his speed. But if he wanted to let one get away . . . maybe if he moved just a bit lazily toward first for a step or two? He would then speed up and seem to be trying hard. But it would be difficult—it would take a suspicious-minded person like Chance—to charge him with anything but an error if a well-thrown peg slipped off the end of his glove."

Lieb also believed that American League officials must have known what Chase was doing, given the comments of Chance and the rumors about Chase that floated among players and journalists. But baseball executives did not want a scandal, so nothing was done. Lieb later argued that this was a serious mistake that led to far greater problems. "Other players," he wrote, "saw Chase get away with it and surely thought, 'Why don't we give it a try?'"

After a stay with the Buffalo team of the short-lived Federal League, Chase joined Cincinnati for the 1916 season. This proved to be his best year. He led the league in batting average at .339 and hits with 184, and he finished second in runs batted in and slugging percentage. Midway through this first season with his new team, Chase found himself with a new manager: Christy Mathewson.

Given the dismal state of the Reds, Mathewson was undoubtedly glad to have Chase, who was the only .300 hitter in his lineup. In

1917, Mathewson's first (and, as it turned out, only) full season as manager, the Reds improved considerably, and Chase carried less of the load. Edd Roush, who had come with Mathewson in the trade from the Giants, led the league with a .341 batting average, third base-man Heinie Groh hit .304, and left fielder Greasy Neale hit a career-high .294. The pitching staff featured two 20-game-winners, and the team climbed from its 60-93 seventh place finish in 1916 to fourth place, with a 78-76 record. (McGraw's Giants won the pennant.) Apparently Mathewson was doing something right.

Chase had tailed off to a .277 average, and despite his reputation as a fine fielder, he committed 28 errors, more than any other major league first baseman that year. That may have caught Mathewson's eye.

In 1918, the Reds were finally a decent team, but Mathewson was dismayed by Chase's flaws in the field. He particularly noticed how often Chase made poor throws to pitchers who covered first when grounders were hit wide of the bag. Mathewson, an excellent fielder himself, knew that this was a fundamental play, practiced over and over. It didn't make sense that Chase could mess it up so often.

In early August, Mathewson learned that Chase had approached a Giants pitcher, Pol Perritt, and offered him a bribe to let Cincinnati beat New York that day. Mathewson had already been gathering evidence against Chase, and now he acted. He suspended Chase for "indifferent playing," and told reporters: "We are trying hard to finish in the first division with a chance of slipping into third place. Our pitching staff is very weak and we need the most earnest work on the part of every player on the team. I will not stand for indifferent or careless playing on the part of a man of such great natural ability as Hal possesses. I think a layoff will do him good."

Although Mathewson implied to reporters that he might lift the suspension, he presented Reds owner Garry Herrmann with his evidence and Herrmann made it clear that Chase was finished with the Cincinnati team.

"This is a case which will bear searching investigation,"

Herrmann said. "Matty is sure that he has the goods on Chase and we will go to the limit to find out the exact truth with regard to his actions in certain games. It is a shame that a player of such great ability and brilliant qualifications should fail to give his best efforts on all occasions. He will never play another game of ball for us, and I rather think that his baseball career is completely over."

Chase didn't think so. He filed suit against the Reds to recover the rest of his season's salary ($1,650) and vowed to clear his name. His teammates, however, didn't leap to his defense. The *Cincinnati Enquirer* reported that "a number of players have felt for some time that there were occasions on which Hal was not exerting himself to the limit of his well known ability." The paper also reported, "It is not a pleasant thing to say about so fine a natural player as Chase, but the other players on the team nearly all have expressed themselves as glad that he is out of the lineup." Although Chase had been hitting .301, the team's play improved after he was replaced.

Chase was not baseball's lone gambler. Ballplayers frequented racetracks and pool halls—John McGraw was part owner of one of each—and other places where bettors and hustlers congregated. Most major leaguers received unspectacular salaries and knew that their careers would be brief, so they were tempted to parlay their earnings into as much as they could get as quickly as possible. Also, betting was in many ways second nature to these men. On train journeys with their teammates, players passed many hours in card games. While on the road and hanging out in hotel lobbies, they would put a few bucks on any attractive wager, and on their days off would head for the track or wherever else they might make some easy money.

With his love of cards, checkers, and other competition, Mathewson was not above all this, but he drew the line at consorting with bookmakers and betting against his own team. Chase, most overtly among his peers, did not observe such boundaries.

Baseball gambling appeared to have grown worse during the 1918 season. A report in *The Sporting News* said that "gambling cliques" based in New York and Boston had been "trying to corrupt big league players all season," and that fifty players had been offered bribes. Baseball officials, sportswriters, and others tried to fix the blame for this outside the game itself. *The Sporting News* editorialized not against all gambling, but just against the most serious cases, such as bribery of players. And the newspaper also found a convenient scapegoat: Jews. An editorial said that the source of the gambling problem was "the pasty-faced and clammy-fingered gentry with the hooked noses."

Despite such transparent anti-Semitism and other efforts to shift blame, Chase, along with several of his teammates, was recognized as a magnet for gambling on ball games. Writer William Phelon said, "The betting grew steadily during the past season in Cincinnati." He wrote about a particular day when he "was astounded at the magnitude of the bets offered on Brooklyn [a relatively weak team] to beat the Reds." On that particular day, Brooklyn *did* beat the Reds, 4-0.

During the summer of 1918, Mathewson and Reds owner Herrmann turned over their findings about Chase to National League president John Heydler. Herrmann understood how explosive the case was, and told Heydler that if Chase were to be expelled from baseball, "the reason for it should not be made public. The evidence is so damaging . . . that it would be a sure black eye for the game if the details became fully known."

On January 30, 1919, Heydler finally held a hearing at which Chase, accompanied by his lawyers, aggressively defended himself. The charges in Mathewson's affidavit, which were severe enough to warrant Chase being banned from baseball, were undercut by none other than John McGraw, who believed that he could keep Chase under control and make him an important part of the Giants lineup. He told Heydler that Chase, if cleared by the league, could come to play in New York. Heydler was nonplussed: "Here I am trying to prove the charges that Mathewson, McGraw's close friend, has made against this man, and McGraw is already offering him a job."

On February 5, Heydler announced his decision clearing Chase:

"It is nowhere established that the accused was interested in any pool or wager that caused any game to result otherwise than on its merits," and he cited a game in which Chase had allegedly bet against the Reds but hit a game-winning home run.

According to the *Cincinnati Enquirer*, Heydler added that "the testimony showed that Chase acted in a foolish and careless manner both on the field and among the players, and that the club was justified in bringing the charges in view of the many rumors which arose from the loose talk of its first baseman. Chase did not take his work seriously and was entirely to blame for the position in which he found himself. There was, however, no proof that he intentionally violated or attempted to violate the rules in relation to tampering with players, or in any way endeavored to secure desired results in the outcome of games. . . . I do not know where Chase will play during the coming season, but I wish to say now that he has been proven not guilty of the charges. I hope the fans and others will give him a fair chance to overcome the unpleasant impression which has been created. . . ."

Despite his official pronouncements, Heydler told Fred Lieb off the record that he believed Chase *was* guilty, "but I have no proof that will stand up in a court of law."

In a testy letter to Herrmann, Heydler expressed his disappointment in the testimony against Chase by Cincinnati pitcher Jimmy Ring, who had claimed that Chase offered him money to let an opposing team win. Heydler said that Ring "was a poor witness and made statements differing from what he had stated in his affidavit. . . . To have found Chase guilty on this man's unsupported testimony would have been impossible." Heydler added, "I feel that it is unfortunate indeed that the Cincinnati club could not in any manner furnish me some direct evidence that Chase had placed a bet against his team," and urged the team to conduct a more thorough investigation on its own if a similar case ever arose.

The Mathewson-versus-Chase battle was not over, but this round went to Chase. A principal reason that the case against the first base-man failed was that the Cincinnati manager's position was presented only on paper. Mathewson, had he appeared in person, certainly would have been a compelling witness. If it had been Mathewson's word against Chase's, Heydler might well have sided with Mathewson.

But on the date of Heydler's hearing, Mathewson was far away.

On August 22, 1918, Mathewson had received the following telegram: "You are appointed Captain, Chemical Warfare Service. Wire accept-ance . . . and proceed ten days after date [to] Washington." Mathewson responded two days later, "Received your telegram notify-ing me of my appointment, which I am pleased to accept."

At age thirty-eight, Mathewson had volunteered to fight in the Great War, joining more than two hundred other Major Leaguers who enlisted, including Ty Cobb, Grover Cleveland Alexander, and George Sisler. For him, as for the country at large, baseball no longer seemed quite so important. He was moving beyond his effort to purge an immoral influence from baseball and responding to President Wilson's call to arms: "The world must be made safe for democracy."

In his speech to Congress on April 2, 1917, Wilson asked for a dec-laration of war and presented his vision of a moral nation's duty: "It is a fearful thing to lead this great peaceful people into war, into the most terrible and disastrous of all wars, civilization itself seeming to be in the balance. But the right is more precious than peace. . . . To such a task we can dedicate our lives and our fortunes, everything that we are and everything that we have, with the pride of those who know that the day has come when America is privileged to spend her blood and her might for the principles that gave her birth and happiness and the peace which she has treasured. God helping her, she can do no other."

Today, such lofty rhetoric sounds archaic. We have become accus-tomed to more prosaic definitions of "the national interest." But in

1917, Wilson's words stirred the nation's sense of honor. Whatever Mathewson may have thought about the larger policy questions concerning America's involvement in the war, it was very much in character for him to respond to Wilson's appeals to patriotism.

Before enlisting, Mathewson had helped the war effort by joining other major leaguers in selling War Savings Stamps. On one occasion in April 1918, he stood on an Oklahoma City street corner to deliver his sales pitch.

"Come on up, you folk, and let's start the game. Remember, Old Man Hindenburg's up to bat and we've got two strikes and one ball against him. Haul out your loose change and help win the pennant in the greatest game ever played, and send that bunch of glass-armed bush leaguers in Berlin back to the bushes."

Mathewson returned to Cincinnati for the first months of the season, but he felt the tug of events. Major league teams continued to play, although Secretary of War Newton Baker had ruled that baseball was a nonessential occupation and therefore ballplayers fell under the "work or fight" policy. This meant that players of draft age, 21–30, had to find jobs "useful in the national defense" or face being drafted into the army. In a compromise between baseball owners and the government, the 1918 season was shortened and the World Series was played in early September.

By that time Mathewson had turned over his manager's job to Heinie Groh, who led the team through its final ten games.

Two weeks after receiving his commission, Mathewson was sent from Washington to New York, where he took time to prepare a list of stocks that he owned (which included shares of U.S. Steel, Westinghouse, and six railroads) and instruct that any future dividends be sent directly to his account at his hometown bank in Lewisburg. He wanted to be sure that his finances were in order and that Jane would be taken care of if he did not return.

He was then ordered to report to Hoboken, New Jersey, "for extended field service." He was vaccinated for typhoid and issued a haversack, canteen, first aid pouch, pistol belt, and other necessities.

By mid-September, he was on his way to France.

SEVEN

Making the World Safe

THE SHIP SAILING to Europe was a British vessel, stripped of its name for security reasons. The newly commissioned Captain Mathewson had to fight off his chronic seasickness, but other than that, life on board was more than tolerable. Among his souvenirs from the voyage was the program from "A Grand Concert" that featured "The Star Spangled Banner," "God Save the King," and "La Marseillaise," as well as a chorus of "It's a Long Way to Berlin," sung by a group of nurses.

It was a pleasant enough Atlantic crossing. Reality, however, awaited. Ten million killed. Twenty million wounded.

Mathewson was part of a massive infusion of American troops pouring into British and French ports in 1918: 245,000 in May, 278,000 in June, 306,000 in July, and still they kept coming, the two million men who served in the American Expeditionary Force. Winston Churchill marveled at this "seemingly inexhaustible flood of gleaming youth" that had arrived to lift up America's allies.

The American troops had been told about this war: that tens of thousands of young men could die during a single day in the blood-soaked mud of the trenches; that artillery and machine guns had made fighting less personal and more devastating; that chemicals were being used to sear skin, eyes, and lungs. They knew about the attack on the Somme in 1916, when, after a weeklong barrage that dropped more than a million shells on the German lines, 110,000 British infantry advanced, and on that one day 60,000 of them were killed or wounded. They knew about Passchendaele in 1917: this time the Allies fired four million shells in ten days to dislodge the Germans, but after three months the battle ended inconclusively, leaving 370,000 British casualties.

Today, Flanders fields are dotted with the results of that fighting: cemeteries, many filled with unidentified remains. The tombstones, row after row of them, read: "A soldier of the Great War. Known unto God." Monuments list the names of the tens of thousands of dead whose bodies were never recovered, obliterated by the incessant shelling and driven deep into the mud.

The Americans had been told what it was like, but they could not appreciate the scope of the butchery until they arrived.

In September, while Mathewson was still at sea, came the Allied victory at St. Mihiel, spearheaded, in Churchill's words, by "the Americans attacking with the utmost ardor." In this and other battles, the late-arriving AEF found plenty of fighting to do, and more than 100,000 Americans lost their lives. But the U.S. forces were fortunate to face a much shorter war than their allies had endured, and most were spared the fear and tedium of spending month after month in the trenches.

By the time many of the Americans, including Mathewson, came ashore, the armistice was little more than a month away. The Americans' presence nevertheless had a major impact on the course of the war. As historian John Keegan observed, "Nowhere among Germany's remaining resources could sufficient force be found to counter the millions America could bring across the Atlantic, and the consequent sense of the pointlessness of further effort rotted the resolution of the ordinary German soldier to do his duty."

Captain Mathewson kept busy. After a brief stop in Liverpool, he arrived in France and was sent to Blois, then to Tours and finally to

Chaumont, about 150 miles southeast of Paris. There he was assigned to the officer training school of the Chemical Warfare Service.

His training had barely begun, however, when influenza, which had been sweeping through the troops, put him in the hospital at Chaumont. He had caught it on the trip over, and it got worse once he landed. After ten days in the hospital, he emerged healthy enough to complete his officer's training, but not at full strength. Still feeling a bit shaky, he moved on to intensive instruction in the Gas Defense School.

The course was short but rigorous, running twelve hours a day for a week. The lectures addressed topics such as "Effects of wind, weather, and topography on gas," and "Investigating a gas shell bombardment." There were also drills in respirator use and first aid.

Despite the brevity of their training, the men of the Chemical Warfare Service were the designated experts on whom the rest of the army relied. They were taught about the array of gases they might have to deal with: phosgene, with its smell of musty hay; ethyl dichlorasine, which was described as smelling "ethereal, pleasant"; and mustard gas, which could linger on a battlefield for three days. Some of the gases the Germans were using were like tear gas, designed to temporarily incapacitate enemy troops, but many others were described as "very deadly."

During the final months of the war, the Germans used gas regularly in the sectors in which Mathewson's Twenty-eighth Division was fighting. According to the division surgeon's casualty report, between July 15 and the November armistice, 3,500 of the division's men were admitted to hospitals due to being gassed. This was 27 percent of the total number hospitalized. Of these, about two-thirds suffered from gas inhalation, and a third from mustard gas burns. During particularly heavy fighting on one September day, 390 men were admitted for gas-related injuries. These numbers reflect only those who were hospitalized; they do not include men who died on the battlefield after being gassed.

After completing his course, Mathewson and his fellow specialists were sent to train American troops to survive and fight during gas attacks. The soldiers received two and a half days of instruction in detecting gas, using respirators, and disinfecting clothing and weapons. Included in this training were drills in which real gas was used. Instructors made certain that the men did not panic and got their respirators on quickly and properly. The instructors were always the last to put on their masks.

There is no record of how many of these drills Mathewson participated in, but in each one he would have been briefly exposed to the gas. Two of his baseball colleagues who also served in the Chemical Warfare Service offered different descriptions of how he fared. Branch Rickey reported that he saw no ill effects, and added that Mathewson would participate in broad jump contests and other athletic events after a day of gas training. Ty Cobb, however, told of a training exercise in which the warning signal for the gas release was given improperly, and everyone was late putting on his mask. According to Cobb, some soldiers died in this accident, and he said that Mathewson told him: "I got a good dose of the stuff. I feel terrible."

Mathewson was not only exposed repeatedly to gas in the exercises, but he also inhaled poisonous fumes when, as part of his job, he inspected trenches and ammunition dumps left behind by retreating Germans. Weakened by his bout with influenza, he was particularly susceptible to the toxic gas. While in France, he fought off its effects, but although he didn't realize it at the time, the gas had done lasting damage.

Mathewson was part of a sizable baseball contingent in the AEF. Facing the "work or fight" rule, team owners had petitioned the Wilson administration for an exemption, arguing that the public would benefit from having the game as a diversion, and—more to the owners' interests—that the teams would face financial disaster if so many players were drafted that games could not be played. Secretary of War Baker responded: "I think it would be an unfortunate thing to have so wholesome a recreation as baseball destroyed. . . . But it would be a much more unfortunate thing to preserve even so wholesome an amusement by making an exception in favor of baseball players which is denied to great numbers of persons in the United States whose occupations have been held similarly nonessential."

And so by war's end more than half of all major leaguers were in uniform, including Burleigh Grimes, Rabbit Maranville, Rube Marquard, Eppa Rixey, and Casey Stengel. Baseball officials proudly noted the sport's contribution to the war effort, including the transfer of ball-throwing skills to grenade hurling. *Spalding's Official Baseball Guide* reported that an unnamed American soldier taught some of his French counterparts how to properly throw a baseball and then had them test their grenade-throwing against others who had not been so trained. The *Guide* noted that "the results were a complete vindication for baseball. The men who had been playing ball threw fully sixty percent farther," and "in the matter of accuracy there was no comparison, the diamond devotees doing immeasurably better work." The effect on the Allies' capabilities in battle was hard to measure, but baseball's officialdom was pleased.

Beyond teaching the fine points of throwing, some ballplayers did see real combat. Among them was Eddie Grant.

Like Mathewson, Edward Leslie Grant was proof that college men could find a place in the big leagues. He was three years younger than Mathewson and had gone to Harvard, where he was captain of the baseball team. He began his ten-year major league career in 1905 and played the infield for four teams. He ended up with the Giants, where he was a useful utility player, batting .277 in 1914.

He was straightforward about playing baseball mainly to fund his education. He told one writer that any athlete doing this "must have the determination never to abandon a fixed policy . . . of being a ballplayer when the playing season is on and a student for the balance of the year." Sticking with this policy gave Grant an off-season profession that few, if any, other professional players could claim. He had used his baseball earnings to pay his tuition for a second Harvard degree, this one from the law school. After seeing limited playing time with the Giants during the 1915 season, he left baseball for good and went into practice.

But other matters held Grant's attention. In May 1915, soon after a German U-boat sank the British passenger liner *Lusitania*, with 124 Americans among the 1,198 passengers killed, he told friends that he believed U.S. intervention was inevitable. When America did enter the war, he volunteered for the army and set out to become an officer.

"I had determined from the start to be in this war if it came to us, and if I am not successful in becoming an officer, I shall enlist as a private, for I believe there is no greater duty that I owe for being that which I am—an American citizen."

He did well in his officer's course and was commissioned a captain in the infantry. His unit was part of the first wave of American troops sent to Europe, and during the fall of 1918 he took part in the fierce battles that raged through northeastern France. In that region, battle lines were often indistinct as fighting surged back and forth through dense forests, and units sometimes seemed to disappear. The most famous of these was "the Lost Battalion."

These 550 Americans found themselves cut off from the rest of the army and surrounded by the enemy in the Argonne Forest north of Verdun. Day after day, they ferociously fought off German attacks while U.S. forces tried to reach them. At one point, American artillery fire mistakenly hit the besieged battalion, and their commander, Major Charles Whittlesey, desperately dispatched his last carrier pigeon, named "Cher Ami," with a message telling the U.S. batteries to shift their fire. Miraculously, the bird made it to the American lines and the barrage was redirected.

Damon Runyon, writing for the *New York American*, reported that Grant's unit had been fighting for four days and nights trying to reach Whittlesey's troops. The soldiers told Runyon that Grant never once slept during that time, and that he constantly moved among them offering encouragement and leading them forward.

On the morning when they were finally about to break through to Whittlesey's beleaguered force, Grant saw his severely wounded commander being carried away on a stretcher, leaving Grant to lead the battalion.

As Grant took over, German artillery fire pierced the forest. Both the unit's remaining lieutenants were badly wounded.

Chaos swirled around him, and Grant shouted to his men: "Everyone get down. Stretcher bearers, you come with me."

While his troops scrambled for cover, Grant stood, waving to the stretcher bearers to show them where the wounded lieutenants were. Then another German shell came screaming down through the trees. A piece of shrapnel ripped into Grant's chest, killing him instantly.

He was the only major leaguer to die in combat during the Great War. The headline on Runyon's story read, "Eddie Grant Sleeps in Argonne Forest."

Mathewson was spared that kind of action, and after the armistice he had a chance to see more of France. As he traveled, he bought postcards that had been quickly produced to show scenes such as French troops entering Metz, a city that Mathewson liked and said he'd like to visit again someday. On one card he wrote, "The American flag shown in the picture was hastily made and had eight stars sewed on one side." Another picture shows Metz residents toppling a statue of Kaiser Wilhelm that had been erected during the German occupation. Mathewson wrote: "How the mighty are fallen! The spectators look pleased that Metz is again a French town. The fathers of some of them fought against the Huns in 1870."

He didn't like everything about Metz. He sent home a menu from the Grand Hotel and wrote, "This was said to be the best meal in Metz. The soup was terrible and the gelée was the color of watermelon. . . ."

By Christmas, he was back at division headquarters, and dinner there proved more satisfying. The fare in the junior officers' mess included lobster salad, roast turkey with oyster stuffing, mince pie, and champagne. From Jane had come a Christmas booklet made by the First Presbyterian Church in Lewisburg and signed by members of his and Jane's families.

Even more pleasing was the memo Mathewson received the next day informing him that he was being relieved and sent to Chinon, beginning, he hoped, a fairly speedy journey back to the States. Most of the ballplayers serving in the armed forces during the war had volunteered rather than waiting to be drafted, and after the armistice they were eager to receive their discharges as quickly as possible so they could get back to the game. Mathewson and many of the other players soon learned how slowly the military bureaucracy can move.

A month after the fighting stopped, Chemical Warfare Service officers were asked by their headquarters to "send in writing any personal or business reasons for return to the States." Mathewson responded immediately.

"My business reason for wishing to return to the United States is that I may be there on or about January 18, 1919, in order to resume my former occupation of managing a National League professional baseball club. Unless at that time I give assurance of being able to accept such a position, I could not find such employment during the season of 1919."

Whether because there were few baseball fans among the army bureaucrats or just not enough transport to carry all the departing Americans, Mathewson's request was ignored. By mid-January, instead of being back with the Cincinnati team, he was in an officers' camp in Angers, southwest of Paris.

This was not a happy place. The soldiers in the camp wanted to go home, and they considered not only the war but the regimentation of military life to be things of the past. As discipline crumbled, newly arriving officers such as Mathewson were given a list of regulations that warned them to behave.

"An officer's conduct and bearing has a direct effect upon his time of departure for embarkation. Up to the date of the publishing of these regulations, the bearing of officers generally has not been satisfactory. Points of criticism and neglect are: Improper uniforms; the wearing of weird and unauthorized styles of top coats; neglect in buttoning uniforms throughout . . . failure to salute a senior officer or to acknowledge his presence or approach by some show of alertness. . . . THIS CARELESSNESS AND THESE NEGLECTS WILL NOT BE PERMITTED."

There followed a lengthy, underlined order about proper saluting, accompanied by warnings not to gamble anywhere in the camp or spit on the floors.

Presumably, Mathewson behaved better than many of his fellow officers, but he was restless and ready to leave France behind. He had been able to get several days leave from camp for a stay in Paris, but as each day passed, he knew that he was more likely to be without a baseball job whenever he finally reached home.

At last, on February 1, he received orders telling him that "your services are no longer required in the A.E.F." and that he was to report to Brest, "ready for immediate embarkation." At 10 A.M. on February 8, he was one of more than 2,700 American soldiers on board the Holland-America Line's S.S. *Rotterdam*, temporarily a troop-ship, as it steamed into the Atlantic.

Mathewson's war was over. He had done his duty, and then some. As a thirty-eight-year-old volunteer, he was an old man among mid-ranking officers. His fellow soldiers in France, like his fans at home, understood that he need not have come.

His was a quiet patriotism. His letters home had a light touch.

There were no somber, Wilsonian pronouncements about affecting the course of world affairs. As in so much of his life, he was just doing what he thought to be the right thing.

Now, he was too impatient to enjoy the voyage home. Too many questions needed answers. Could he get back into baseball? Would anyone want to hire him? Would the fans remember him?

Each day, he paced the deck and jotted down how many nautical miles had been covered. On the morning of February 17, the *Rotterdam* docked in Hoboken, New Jersey.

Reporters were there to greet him. That was a good sign. He handled them smoothly.

"The people over here should thank God that the war wasn't in this country. War is all Sherman said it was, and then some."

The reporters asked whether Mathewson and other Americans had convinced the French of the virtues of baseball.

"Baseball will never be a popular game in France, I'm afraid. The French think it is brutal. They are more afraid of a hard-hit grounder or liner than they are of a German shell. Their infield work is bad. They can run the bases all right, but have little opportunity because they cannot bat. And the thing which the French players absolutely cannot do is to stand up close behind the batsman and catch. They want to retreat about ten yards and catch the ball. I saw a couple of Americans playing ball in the street, and no one would pass behind the catcher. The result was that traffic was held up because those French people were so sure that the catcher would miss the ball and they would get hit."

The reporters laughed along with him. Then they asked about his future in Cincinnati, where a manager had been hired to replace him. He just grinned and said, "I don't know a thing about what's going on in baseball. I'm out of touch with things in that line nowadays." They tried the question again, and he just smiled. No one pressed him.

He later said that he had not received the cablegrams Reds owner Garry Herrmann had sent him. Herrmann had planned to reinstate Mathewson as manager, but when there was no response to his cables, he had recruited former catcher and Philadelphia manager Pat Moran to lead the team.

But when Matty was asked on the Hoboken dock if he'd accept a job with the Giants, he answered quickly. "I was in New York a great many years, and it seems like home to me." That gave the reporters something to chew on.

As he left the ship, the crowd that had been waiting to meet other returning soldiers recognized him and started cheering. He smiled and waved. They did remember.

Christy, Jane and Christy Jr. moved easily back into their comfortable New York life. Jane had spent some of the time during Christy's absence in Lewisburg, but now everything was back to normal. Despite the clamor that accompanied Christy's career, the three of them had always enjoyed just being quietly together. Now they had that again, and almost everything was perfect.

The only problem was the cough he had brought back from France. He couldn't shake it. His doctor told him it was chronic bronchitis; a nuisance, nothing more.

While he settled in at home, Mathewson wasted no time in freeing himself from various obligations. First, he went to Washington, where he was given his honorable discharge. Next, he arranged to be officially released by Cincinnati. Then came the step he had been looking forward to: He joined the Giants as coach and John McGraw's heir apparent. His old friend and former manager was not coy about the future.

"Two or three years more, maybe before that, are as long as I'm likely to be out on the field managing, and I don't know a better man who could be found to succeed me than Matty. It was in New York he made his reputation, and I've always considered him part of our organization here. I am immensely pleased that he will coach for me, and it will please me just as much to see him manager of the Giants when the time comes."

Matty was back in baseball. The future was shining.

The nation's future was more problematic. America emerged from the war relatively unscathed and with a new role as the dominant international power. But many Americans were wary about engagement with the rest of the world. As Woodrow Wilson discovered, public opinion could be more easily rallied to support a war than to ensure a peace. On a grueling, 8,000-mile train journey across America, the president took his idealistic and cautionary message to the people.

He said that making the League of Nations an effective tool for maintaining peace would be "the test of the honor and courage and endurance of the world." Speaking of the children he saw crowding around the presidential train, he said: "I know that if by any chance we should not win this great fight for the League of Nations it would be their death warrant. They belong to the generation that would have to fight the final war [in which] the very existence of civilization would be in the balance."

But Wilson's vision of a new world order was no match for the pragmatists, cynics, and partisan politicians arrayed against it. The adulation of crowds who came to hear his plea did not change minds in Washington. His tour ended when he suffered a stroke, and his dream died when he was unable to win Senate ratification of the peace treaty, partly because he refused to compromise.

As the United States stepped back into what proved to be brief isolation, life at home was changing. America had wealth and power, but lacked a sense of purpose. The system was out of synch, as evidenced by Prohibition, which was expanding state by state before becoming a Constitutional mandate. The measure would prove that wrapping an unpopular and largely unenforceable law in a cloak of morality was not enough to make it successful.

For some in the postwar period, life was a yo-yo, moving back and forth between high spirits and malaise. The most adroit chronicler of these days was a college dropout whose novels featured characters both beautiful and flawed.

F. Scott Fitzgerald was sixteen years younger than Mathewson, and given the nature of their times, this meant they were of very different generations. Mathewson's fame was established before the Great War; Fitzgerald was the novelist laureate of the Jazz Age that followed it.

They did, however, both serve in the army during the war. Fitzgerald was commissioned as a second lieutenant in October 1917, and his first soldierly act was to go to New York to be fitted for a uniform at Brooks Brothers. The paths of the two men almost crossed at Camp Sheridan in Montgomery, Alabama. Before the 1918 season began, Mathewson offered a pitching clinic to soldiers at the base as part of baseball's support for the war effort. Fitzgerald arrived several months after Mathewson's visit and promptly fell in love with Montgomery belle Zelda Sayre, whom he married two years later.

Training camp was as close to the war as Fitzgerald would get. Fitzgerald biographer Arthur Mizener wrote that Fitzgerald at this time was "getting on with his career as the worst second lieutenant in the army." He was also working on a book he titled *The Romantic Egotist*. Much revised, it became *This Side of Paradise*, which historian Mark Sullivan called "an opening gun in the pro-youth, pro-freedom, and anti-Puritan campaign." Published in 1920, the novel reflected a mix of disillusionment and hedonism. Gertrude Stein wrote that the book had "really created for the public the new generation."

In a 1937 article, Fitzgerald looked back at his first days of fame.

"America was going on the greatest, gaudiest spree in history and there was going to be plenty to tell about it. The whole golden boom was in the air—its splendid generosities, its outrageous corruptions and the tortuous death struggle of the old America in prohibition. All the stories that came into my head had a touch of disaster in them. . . . For my point of vantage was the dividing line between the two generations, and there I sat—somewhat self-consciously."

Self-conscious or not, Fitzgerald painted, in *This Side of Paradise*, a portrait of the rising postwar generation. He depicted his contemporaries as "destined finally to go out into that dirty gray turmoil to follow love and pride; a new generation dedicated more than the last to the fear of poverty and the worship of success; grown up to find all Gods dead, all wars fought, all faiths in man shaken. . . ."

The demarcation Fitzgerald defined was not based solely on experience in the war. He had written as early as 1917 that everyone he had met who had gone to fight "seems to have lost youth and faith in man," but by war's end he understood that bigger changes were occurring, a result of pervasive uncertainty. In the final sentence of *This Side of Paradise*, his alter ego Amory Blaine cries out, "I know myself, but that is all." A bit histrionic, to be sure, but an accurate reflection of the longing for lost innocence that would accompany his generation's unsure march into the future.

This was the America in which Mathewson returned to baseball. McGraw and others in the sport welcomed him back as a symbol of prewar glory and postwar continuity. He was still baseball's biggest star, and his presence in the Giants dugout was expected to stir fans' memories and bring them back to the ballpark.

The Giants had finished second, behind Chicago, in the abbreviated 1918 season, and McGraw was intent on rebuilding. He began by changing spring training sites, moving from Marlin, Texas, to Gainesville, Florida. McGraw, Mathewson and the rest of the Giants were welcomed as celebrities in Gainesville, and a local newspaper reported that "every possible courtesy will be shown Manager McGraw and the Giants, and the welcome program arranged in their honor lacks nothing." The University of Florida's string band was on hand at the train station to greet the arriving team, and after a welcome-to-Gainesville dinner, a forty-car procession took the players to the university field so they could inspect the diamond where they would play. The mayor declared the day of an exhibition game versus the Boston Red Sox a holiday, and he requested that all businesses close to allow people to go to the game.

Another change McGraw made was to acquire a new first baseman: Hal Chase. McGraw was desperate for added punch in his lineup and, ever the pragmatist, he ignored the case Mathewson had made against Chase the previous year and accepted Chase's promise that he had done nothing wrong. McGraw dismissed the possibility of conflict between his new coach and Chase, telling reporters: "I didn't give the matter any thought. It doesn't give me the slightest concern. Neither is necessary to the other, and each is smart enough to overlook things." Mathewson proved he could continue to be a good soldier, publicly claiming that he had no unfriendly feelings toward Chase.

The specifics of Chase's misbehavior in Cincinnati were known to only a few, McGraw among them. The baseball writers knew all the rumors about unsavory activity, but they also knew that Chase's talent was undeniable. For their part, Giants fans were ready to overlook Chase's moral shortcomings as long as his skill at the plate and in the field would win games for the Giants. It was assumed that regardless of Chase's reputation, McGraw could keep him in line.

But the peace between Mathewson and Chase was an uneasy one. They wouldn't speak to each other, and other players noted the tension between the two men. On one occasion, a bat slipped out of Larry Doyle's hands and hit Mathewson in the stomach during pregame warmups. Most of the players rushed to Matty's side. Chase just stood and watched.

Whenever he was questioned by reporters about Chase, Mathewson retreated into platitudes. If he had complaints about Chase, McGraw was the only one to hear them.

The 1919 National League pennant race was between two teams: the Giants and the surprising Cincinnati Reds. Pat Moran, after inheriting Mathewson's job with the Reds, had added a few players and assembled a winner. By late summer, Cincinnati was pulling away from New York and Chase's play was becoming more erratic. In a crucial August series between the Giants and the Reds, Chase committed a number of damaging errors.

Finally, the crisis came to a head. After the first inning of a game against Chicago, pitcher Fred Toney went to Mathewson, who was in charge of working with the Giants pitchers, and asked to be replaced. Toney later told McGraw that Heinie Zimmerman, the Giants third baseman who had won the Triple Crown in 1912, had approached him on the field and offered him $200 to lose. Toney didn't want to have anything to do with a crooked game.

McGraw suspended Zimmerman, and then word filtered through the clubhouse that Zimmerman and Chase had been working together, offering bribes to players who might help throw games. McGraw let Chase, whom he liked personally, remain with the team until the end of the season, but Chase was finished as a major league player.

National League president John Heydler later told journalist Fred Lieb that he had finally found the solid evidence against Chase that was not available during the investigation into Mathewson's 1918 charges. Heydler had received a signed affidavit from a Boston gambler and a canceled check for $500 that the gambler had paid to Chase for throwing a game. Heydler took this new evidence to Giants owner Charles Stoneham and told him that Chase must not be allowed to play again.

Finally, Mathewson was vindicated. After instigating the case against Chase while in Cincinnati, Mathewson undoubtedly found it difficult being with the Giants and watching Chase play every day. It could be argued that he should have forced McGraw's hand, demanding that McGraw choose between him and the first baseman. But McGraw wanted to win another pennant and thought he needed Chase to have a chance. Mathewson knew he could push McGraw only so far, and taking into account his own desire to become the next Giants manager, he backed off, perhaps realizing that Chase would eventually self-destruct. In any event, despite being outmaneuvered in several battles, Mathewson finally won the war.

The banishment of Chase was a victory for baseball as Mathewson thought it should be played. But soon the game would be tested even more severely, and both Mathewson and Chase would again be involved.

EIGHT

Fading Away

> "He's a gambler." Gatsby hesitated, then added coolly: "He's the man who fixed the World's Series back in 1919."
>
> "Fixed the World's Series?" I repeated.
>
> The idea staggered me. I remembered of course that the World's Series had been fixed in 1919, but if I had thought of it at all I would have thought of it as a thing that merely happened, the end of some inevitable chain. It never occurred to me that one man could start to play with the faith of fifty million people—with the single-mindedness of a burglar blowing a safe.
>
> "How did he happen to do that?" I asked after a minute.
>
> "He just saw the opportunity."
>
> —F. Scott Fitzgerald,
> The Great Gatsby

THAT'S HOW IT WAS. Gambler Arnold Rothstein—Meyer Wolfsheim in Fitzgerald's novel—saw the opportunity presented by ballplayers willing to sell out their game and themselves.

Mathewson watched this take place and, at first, simply refused to admit to anyone that it could happen. Despite what he'd gone through with Hal Chase, he could not bring himself to think that his game, the country's game, could be so thoroughly corrupted.

But as he watched, he knew.

For Mathewson 1919 had been a strange year, beginning in France, continuing with his return to baseball as a Giants coach, and culminating in autumn with a World Series at which he was something of an outsider. He had come as a journalist, working for the New York *World*, an observer instead of a player. It felt very strange.

Baseball had done well in 1919. The season had started late, as troops slowly made their way home. Each team scheduled only 140 games, but attendance more than doubled from its wartime low, climbing above 6.5 million. Stars were shining: Ty Cobb continued his torrid hitting, ending the season at .384, and a Boston Red Sox outfielder-pitcher named Babe Ruth hit a remarkable 29 home runs.

Even in the days before television, the World Series was a full-scale media circus, and Mathewson was out of his element. He stayed close to his pal Hugh Fullerton, a sportswriter for the Chicago *Herald and Examiner*. Fullerton knew things were going wrong. He was surprised by the volume and consistency of the rumors: the fix was in; the heavily favored White Sox were going in the tank, so get your money on Cincinnati.

Another Chicago journalist, James Crusinberry of the *Tribune*, told how he too was shaken awake. He recalled walking into the Sinton Hotel in Cincinnati the day before the Series began, where he saw "a man standing on a chair—his hands filled with paper money—calling for wagers on the ball games. The man was Abe Attell, former featherweight boxing champion of the world.

"I walked up close to him. He was waving big money. There were $1,000 bills between the fingers of both hands and he was yelling in a loud voice that he would cover any amount of Chicago money. I was amazed. I had never seen anything like that before in any World Series, nor have I seen anything like it since. The man was eager to wager thousands of dollars on the underdog. I couldn't understand it. I felt that something was wrong, almost unbelievably wrong."

Something had to be wrong, because there was no way that people were going to bet against the White Sox, unless they couldn't resist longshots. The Sox were led by Shoeless Joe Jackson and Eddie Collins, who had batted .351 and .319 respectively during the season.

The pitching staff featured Eddie Cicotte, who had gone 29-7 with a 1.82 ERA, and Lefty Williams, who went 23-11 with an ERA of 2.64.

Cincinnati was not a bad team. Under Pat Moran's leadership, the Reds had piled up 96 wins (eight more than the White Sox had won) and their lineup featured National League batting champ Edd Roush. Three Reds pitchers—Hod Eller, Dutch Ruether, and Slim Sallee—had put together a combined record of 60-22. Before the Series began, no less an observer than John McGraw predicted that pitching would be "at least 65 percent" and that Cincinnati had a deeper staff than Chicago. The new best-of-nine Series format, said McGraw, "should favor Cincinnati."

But during the season, the White Sox had run up an exceptional team batting average of .287—Cincinnati's was .263—and McGraw's observations aside, the conventional wisdom was that no pitching staff could withstand the onslaught of Shoeless Joe and company.

The Series began October 1 in Cincinnati, and the rumors continued to swirl. Fullerton asked Mathewson how a game could be thrown. Matty explained the tiny margin of error for every pitch and swing of the bat and play in the field. Could that fastball have been an inch farther away from the batter? Could the hitter have started his swing a fraction of a second earlier? Might the outfielder's near-miss of the bloop hit have been a catch if he had sprinted just a bit harder? No one could answer such questions with certainty, and no ballplayer or sportswriter would dare try.

Nevertheless, a certain level of play could be expected. In the first game, Chicago's Eddie Cicotte fielded a ball hit back to the mound. He was in good shape to turn it into a pitcher-to-second-to-first double play. But he was slow getting the ball to second, and he threw it just a touch high, allowing the force out to be made but leaving shortstop Swede Risberg with an awkward throw to first. The Reds batter beat it by a step.

It was a play that gets made, not muffed, by a prospective world champion. In the press box, Mathewson and Fullerton agreed that it didn't look right.

Even as the bottom of the Cincinnati batting order clobbered Cicotte, Mathewson remained willing to give his fellow pitcher the benefit of the doubt. It was just one of those days, he told Fullerton.

Cincinnati won four of the first five games, and then Chicago came to life, winning the next two. With the Reds' lead in the Series cut to 4-3 and the White Sox apparently resurgent, talk of a fix quieted. Fullerton and Mathewson still had their doubts about the performance of some of the Chicago players, but lacking evidence beyond instinct they were willing to write off the errors and bad pitches to World Series nerves or other unintentional lapses.

But as he arrived at Comiskey Park for the eighth game—the chance for Chicago to tie the Series—Fullerton was approached by a gambler who told him to watch for "the biggest first inning you ever saw."

Chicago's Lefty Williams had already lost two games, but he had pitched decently, giving up four runs in each of his eight-inning stints.

As the game began, he won cheers from the Chicago fans as he threw a first-pitch strike past Maury Rath. Then a foul ball. Then a pop-up to shortstop Risberg. A good start for the White Sox.

Then Jake Daubert hit a flare into center for a single. Heinie Groh was next; he lined a single to right.

Mathewson saw what was happening. So far, Williams was throwing only fastballs. The Cincinnati hitters spotted this and dug in. Catcher Ray Schalk went out to the mound and told Williams to mix up his pitches.

Then, another fastball. Edd Roush smashed a double to right, and Daubert scored the game's first run. Schalk yelled at Williams, and Chicago manager Kid Gleason signaled the bullpen to get going, now.

Pat Duncan stepped up and got the fastball he expected. He smashed it into left for a single, driving in two more runs.

Williams got a strike past Larry Kopf. But it was another fastball. Gleason came charging out of the dugout, yelling at Williams and motioning to the bullpen for Bill James to take over.

Williams walked slowly off the field. He had gotten one man out, while surrendering three runs on four hits. He had thrown fifteen pitches, all fastballs.

The game and the Series ended with a 10-5 Cincinnati victory. Mathewson knew that he had just seen baseball suffer a body blow. Gleason and White Sox owner Charles Comiskey also realized what had happened, but they had no proof. Publicly, they kept quiet.

But not Fullerton. In the next day's *Herald and Examiner*, he wrote: "There will be a great deal written and talked about this World's Series. There will be a lot of inside stuff that never will be printed. . . . Almost everything went backward, so much so that an evil-minded person might believe the stories that have been circulated during the series." Choosing his words carefully, Fullerton said the White Sox had failed to play together as a team, and added, "It is not up to me to decide why they did such things. That all probably will come out in the wash." He prophesied that this would be the last World Series, and that seven members of the White Sox would not be with the team or even in baseball by the following spring.

But the baseball establishment was circling the wagons. Fullerton's comments drew withering criticism from *The Sporting News*, which denounced "stories that were peddled that there was something wrong with the games." The paper leveled an anti-Semitic tirade against "dirty, long-nosed, thick-lipped, and strong-smelling gamblers" who had "butted into the World Series." Whatever problems may have arisen had been caused by outsiders, said the paper, not by anyone within baseball.

That was only partly true. Gamblers may have been the instigators, but they could accomplish nothing without the cooperation of crooked players. Even honest players found themselves being approached by gamblers who seemed to assume that ballplayers could be bought. During the same Series, Cincinnati's Edd Roush was told by an acquaintance that some of the Reds players were in gamblers' pockets. Roush told manager Pat Moran, who raised the issue at a team meeting. Moran turned to pitcher Hod Eller, who was to start that day's game five.

"Has anybody offered you anything to throw this game?"

"Yep."

Everyone in the locker room froze.

"After breakfast this morning a guy got on the elevator with me and got off at the same floor I did. He showed me five thousand-dollar bills, and said they were mine if I'd lose the game today."

"What did you say?"

"I said if he didn't get damn far away from me real quick he wouldn't know what hit him. And the same went if I ever saw him again."

Moran stared at Eller. Finally he said, "Okay, you're pitching. But one wrong move and you're out of the game."

Eller pitched a three-hit shutout, striking out nine.

In the midst of the Black Sox scandal was none other than Hal Chase. Mathewson made no public comment about this, but he could scarcely have been surprised. He knew that gamblers were infesting baseball, and men like Hal Chase welcomed opportunities to do their bidding.

The extent of Chase's involvement in the 1919 Series fix is not known. He has been accused of orchestrating the entire scheme by linking the gamblers and the players, which is plausible but seems a more complicated task than he would undertake. More likely, he knew of the fix, got his bets down, and tipped his cronies to it.

In 1920, an Illinois grand jury indicted eight White Sox players and five gamblers, including Chase, on conspiracy charges stemming from the Series. Chase was arrested in California, where he was living, but went free because of a flaw in the warrant. He, like the other gamblers, slipped out of the picture as the trial of the Black Sox players proceeded, ending with their acquittal.

During an interview a month before his death in 1947, Chase said that his "most costly error" was his failure to notify baseball officials that the Series was being rigged. He admitted that gambler Lefty Burns had approached him before the Series to get his help in organizing the fix, but he said that he had turned him down. Chase said, "I never received a cent from any player or gambler. . . . My name was tossed around and I received much of the blame for plotting the fix. That is a lie, but . . . no one wanted to believe my story."

Other accounts portray Chase as far less innocent. According to some, he won tens of thousands of dollars in bets that he placed after learning the details of the plot. At the time of the Series, the word was out that Chase was betting heavily on Cincinnati, and no one believed it was because of sentimental attachment to his former team.

Although he was able to avoid the Black Sox trial, Chase would never again find a home in major league baseball. He played semipro ball in Arizona, teaming up briefly with Black Sox outcasts Chick Gandil and Buck Weaver. Then he faded into the mists of what might have been. In memory, his talent rightly remains overshadowed by the contempt he showed for the honor of the game.

Well before the Black Sox Series, gambling was recognized as more than just a problem with individual miscreants such as Chase. Rather, it was a pervasive threat to baseball's integrity.

Even baseball books for young readers used gamblers as stock villains and their schemes as threats to the ball-playing heroes. Gilbert Patten, who as Burt Standish created the Frank and Dick Merriwell series and other sports books for young people, used gambling in his plots. In *Guarding the Keystone Sack*, published in 1917 as part of "The Big League" series, hero Lefty Locke must fend off a crooked rival for his manager's job and match wits with a gambler who relies on extortion and kidnapping among other tactics. Lefty, the team's star pitcher as well as manager, prevails, of course, but the lesson from this and other popular baseball novels was that gambling was a serious menace that threatened to undermine the virtues the game should reflect.

The powerful men who ran baseball understood this. Some feared for the future of sportsmanship; others were more concerned about jeopardized profits. They appreciated Mathewson as a personification of the virtue they liked to advertise, but they also knew that to defend the game, they needed someone far more combative and powerful than the retired pitcher. Even if it meant ceding some of their carefully protected authority, they decided to convince the public that baseball was going to be cleaned up.

Judge Kenesaw Mountain Landis was a devoted baseball fan, a partisan of the Chicago Cubs. While still practicing law before going to the bench, he asked an opposing lawyer: "Can't we get a postponement of the case until tomorrow? Brownie [Mordecai Brown] is pitching against Matty, and I just can't miss that." As a federal judge, he told Marquette University law students in 1909 that "no intelligent man doubts the integrity of baseball." He added, "There is no gambling connected with baseball, and I am glad of it, for it is certainly a wholesome sport. It is a compliment to the nation to love such a clean and thoroughly wholesome sport."

Although his appraisal of baseball at that time was grounded more in wishful thinking than in fact, he was normally a tough realist. Before he turned his attention to baseball's problems a month after the 1919 Series, he hammered out a deal with club owners to get the authority and salary he wanted. There was much threatening and cajoling during the negotiations, but Landis emerged triumphant. That the owners gave in was itself a revolutionary change for baseball.

His outlook on the game was similar to Mathewson's, the main difference being that Landis had the power to police the sport. His basic standard, which he defined when banning the Black Sox players who had been acquitted in court, was this: "Regardless of the verdict of juries, no player that throws a ball game, no player that undertakes or promises to throw a ball game, no player that sits in a conference with a bunch of crooked players and gamblers where the ways and means of throwing games are planned and discussed and does not promptly tell his club about it, will ever play professional baseball. . . . Just keep in mind, regardless of the verdict of juries, baseball is entirely competent to protect itself against crooks, both inside and outside the game."

He applied this standard when White Sox infielder Buck Weaver applied for reinstatement. Weaver claimed that although he had sat in on meetings when the Series-fixing conspiracy was planned, he had not participated, as his performance in the Series proved. (He batted .324 and committed no errors.) Landis did not relent: "Birds of a feather flock together. Men associating with gamblers and crooks could expect no leniency."

Landis did not stop with the Black Sox. He declared war on gamblers, whom he denounced as "vermin" who would "sell out their mothers or the Virgin Mary." They wanted, he said, to get "their slimy fingers around baseball, but, by God, so long as I have anything to do with this game they'll never get another hold on it." After addressing the Black Sox case, he expelled seven other players and suspended thirty-eight more during the next four years.

Landis's standards were soon incorporated within baseball's official rules. A section addressing "Conduct Detrimental to Baseball" spoke to any player "who shall promise or agree to lose, or fail to give his best efforts toward the winning of any baseball game . . . or who shall solicit or attempt to induce any player" to throw a game, or who, if so solicited, "shall fail to inform his league president and the commissioner immediately." These players, said the rules, "shall be declared permanently ineligible." Similar rules applied to tampering with umpires. Concerning direct involvement with gambling, if a player bet on a baseball game in which he was not playing, he could be suspended for a year. If he bet on a game in which he *was* playing, he could be permanently banned.

Despite Landis's efforts, baseball has never totally escaped gambling-related controversy. The honesty of great players such as Ty Cobb and Tris Speaker has been questioned. Baseball commissioner Bowie Kuhn banned Willie Mays in 1979 and Mickey Mantle in 1983 because they worked as greeters at Atlantic City casinos. They were both reinstated in 1985. The most celebrated recent banishment was that of all-time hits leader Pete Rose in 1989, after Commissioner A. Bartlett Giamatti found that he had bet on baseball games.

In a statement released to the press just a week before his death, Giamatti addressed his decision to ban Rose. He promised to use "every lawful and ethical means to defend and protect the game." He said that baseball "must assert and aspire to the highest principles—of integrity, of professionalism of performance, of fair play within its rules." Giamatti noted that while no institution is perfect, baseball, "because it is so much a part of our history as a people and because it has such a purchase on our national soul, has an obligation to the people for whom it is played—to its fans and well-wishers—to strive for excellence in all things and to promote the highest ideals."

Giamatti vowed vigilance, vigor and patience "in protecting the game from blemish or stain or disgrace." He concluded by saying that "no individual is superior to the game."

When Mathewson brought his case against Hal Chase and then watched the deeds of the Black Sox, there was no Landis or Giamatti with the authority and willingness to give Mathewson's standards the force of law within baseball. He stood alone, and as a result he was deeply disappointed. He could only watch while the game suffered.

As evidence of a fix piled up during the 1919 Series, he told Hugh Fullerton that the earlier failure to act against Hal Chase had set a disastrous precedent and had led to the undermining of the World Series. Mathewson angrily said of baseball's rulers: "They deserve it! They whitewashed one case and invited it."

Idealism appeared ill-suited to the gaudy amorality of postwar America. Mathewson came away from the 1919 Series saddened and exhausted.

And his cough wouldn't go away.

In spring training and through the beginning of the 1920 season, the Giants got off to a good start. Mathewson was on the field every day, hitting fly balls for outfield practice and working with the pitchers. He later said, "I felt fine, slept well, had a good appetite, and weighed 185 pounds stripped." But as the team traveled from city to city in June, his cough hung on, as did a clogged feeling in his chest and a shortness of breath when he climbed stairs.

When the Giants were in Chicago, he went to a doctor there. The verdict: "Bronchial trouble." In Boston, another doctor: "Heavy cold." Finally, back in New York, a doctor suggested a sputum test. It came back positive, indicating active tuberculosis.

Despite the fact that his brother Henry had died of tuberculosis just three years earlier, Mathewson was not terribly concerned. He had always been healthy and assumed that a six-week rest cure would take care of the problem. Mathewson's doctor suggested that he go to Saranac Lake, New York, a center of tuberculosis treatment, for a more complete examination. Unworried, Mathewson made the trip alone, expecting to return to New York shortly.

Today tuberculosis seems a remote problem to most Americans. Currently eight million people develop TB and three million die each year, mostly in underdeveloped nations. In the United States, with good treatment available, there are about 15,000 cases of TB and 900 deaths from the disease annually. But in 1920, when the U.S. population was slightly more than a third of what it is today, more than 100,000 Americans died of TB. Worldwide during the nineteenth century, tuberculosis killed 14 percent of the human race.

When Mathewson reached Saranac Lake, his nonchalance quickly dissolved. He saw a tuberculosis specialist and was given a harsh prognosis: Both lungs were infected and he might have less than six weeks to live. Jane and Christy Jr. soon joined him, and he began his battle.

Saranac Lake owes its existence to a single industry—the treatment of tuberculosis. This industry evolved from the work of one man, Dr. Edward Livingston Trudeau, whose efforts in medicine were comparable to those of Henry Ford in automobile manufacturing. Not that Trudeau treated his patients in assembly line fashion. To the contrary, he was renowned for his generosity and kindness, and for the individualized attention he gave to those who were ill. But, like Ford, he took his ideas about how things should be done and developed a system that came to be accepted throughout America and elsewhere as the best hope at that time for combating TB.

As a young physician in New York City, Trudeau was diagnosed with tuberculosis in 1872. He traveled in search of a place where his lungs could mend and found relief only in upstate New York's Adirondack Mountains. The air there is exceptionally dry, due in part to the sandy, porous soil that retains little moisture. A local history notes that "papers and books can be left in a summer camp all winter without showing a trace of dampness in the spring."

With his health getting better, he settled in the hamlet of Saranac Lake, in the midst of the Adirondacks, in 1876. Other physicians, learning of Trudeau's improvement, sent their tubercular patients to Saranac Lake, where a twenty-room hotel was built to accommodate them.

Trudeau spent much of his time hunting and fishing, but he also kept up with his medical journals. In 1882, he read about two important breakthroughs: Robert Koch's identification of the tubercle bacillus, and the work at two German sanatoria where tuberculosis patients were placed on a tightly supervised regimen of rest and fresh air. Koch's discovery inspired Trudeau to undertake his own laboratory work, and the sanatoria plan led him to create a facility for people who could not afford to rent houses in town.

After raising money from wealthy patients and friends, he bought land and started work on some small cottages. By 1884, the first cottage was ready and the first patients—two sisters who were "factory girls"—arrived. The Adirondack Cottage Sanitarium was open.

Using the tubercle bacillus that he had cultured in his laboratory, Trudeau conducted experiments on rabbits that produced results supporting his theories about the value of exposure to fresh air. He never claimed to have found a cure that would work in every case, and he tried to admit only patients who had been diagnosed in the early stages of the disease. Sanitarium patients were charged five dollars per week for board and lodging, and fifty cents per dozen pieces for laundry. Everything else, including all doctors' services, was free.

Patients flocked to the sanitarium and to rental cottages in the village. In October 1887, writer Robert Louis Stevenson arrived, rented a cottage, and was treated by Trudeau. While in Saranac Lake, Stevenson wrote most of *The Master of Ballantrae*, a dozen essays for *Scribner's* magazine, and other items.

He was not a model patient. Trudeau told of finding Stevenson not resting, as he was supposed to, but writing in bed, his head propped up by pillows, his knees pulled up to serve as a writing desk, a pencil in one hand, a cigarette in the other. His room was invariably overheated and filled with tobacco smoke, just the opposite of what Trudeau had prescribed.

Nevertheless, the two men became good friends. Stevenson gave Trudeau a fifteen-volume set of his works, with a rhymed dedication

in each book. In *Dr. Jekyll and Mr. Hyde*, for example, the inscription
read:

> Trudeau was all winter at my side!
> I never spied the nose of Mr. Hyde.

The sanitarium kept growing. What began as one building on 16
acres eventually became 58 buildings on 85 acres. The popularity of
the sanitarium method was growing as well. In 1884, Trudeau's
establishment was the only one of its kind. By 1909, there were 352
private and state institutions based on Trudeau's model. Several of
these were in the Saranac Lake area, including a center run by the
National Vaudeville Artists Fund, which eventually became known as
the Will Rogers Hospital.

In addition to having its economy boosted by the services required
at the sanitarium, Saranac Lake was enjoying a construction boom.
"Cure cottages"—homes built or renovated for patients—were
springing up around town. Their distinguishing feature was the cure
porch, an unheated room—often with sliding windows—in which a
patient could rest in the fresh air while remaining within the house.

Although he expanded his staff to administer the sanitarium and
care for his patients, Trudeau himself remained the guiding spirit of
tuberculosis treatment in America. His credo was, "To cure sometimes, to relieve often, to comfort always." He appreciated the value
of hope. His patients often found that even their families and friends
had given them up for lost. At the sanitarium, members of the staff—
many of them former patients—understood the psychological com-
ponent of treatment, so optimism was everywhere.

The optimism was not always well-founded. Despite the dedication of Trudeau and his colleagues, the treatment's success was
limited. One study of the sanitarium's former patients found that 66
percent of those who had begun treatment during the earliest stages
of the disease stayed well. But only 29 percent of those with advanced

stages at admission and just 3 percent of people with far advanced cases remained well. Trudeau reminded the readers of this study that these numbers reflected the reality of tuberculosis.

Trudeau's own long-lingering tuberculosis finally killed him at age sixty-seven in 1915. The Adirondack Cottage Sanitarium was renamed the Trudeau Sanatorium, and Trudeau's work was carried on by his son Francis and his grandson Francis Jr. (His great-grandson Garry pursued a nonmedical career, creating "Doonesbury.")

By 1954, tuberculosis treatment had been changed radically by the introduction of isoniazid and other drugs. Rest and fresh air were no longer the best responses to the disease, so Dr. Francis Trudeau closed the sanatorium. As the facility shut down, the last patient to depart was Christy Mathewson's teammate Larry Doyle, who had recovered well from his own tuberculosis. He stayed on in Saranac Lake and helped launch the Matty League for young ballplayers. He died there in 1974 at age eighty-seven.

Dr. Francis Trudeau Jr. established the Trudeau Institute as successor to the sanatorium. This research center focuses on immunology and cancer as well as tuberculosis and other infectious diseases. It too is located in Saranac Lake, just a few miles from Edward Trudeau's original site.

Today, the old Trudeau Sanatorium is like a medical ghost town. Some of its buildings are crumbling, and the windows of cure porches are shattered. But the mountain air and glorious views are still invigorating, and the spirit of the place remains. If you walk amongst the cottages, with only the Adirondack breeze to keep you company, you can sense the power of hope that nurtured the thousands who lived here years ago.

Mathewson's sudden departure from the Giants at the beginning of July 1920 was accompanied by an announcement that he was retiring from baseball. No precise information about the state of his health was provided beyond some references to an aggravated case of bronchitis. This was an era when public figures were accorded some privacy.

A week after he left for Saranac Lake, the *New York Herald* editorialized that "the qualities of character Mathewson displayed outside of his professional skill were widely recognized. . . . The simplicity and genuineness of his disposition, his unaffected candor, his natural devotion to clean living, and his high conception of right conduct enabled him to impress the desirability of manly virtues and fine ideals on many youngsters. . . ." The editorial concluded with "the good wishes of all for his future prosperity."

By the end of July, the word was out. The *New York Times* ran a story headlined "Matty's Illness Is Tuberculosis." The report noted that Mathewson was "confined to his room" and "undergoing absolute rest."

In December, rumors fed news reports about Mathewson's condition. A *Times* story headlined "Matty Is Making Battle for Life" said that he had suffered a serious relapse, was suffering great pain while coughing, and was unable to leave his bed. Jane told a reporter that "there is absolutely nothing to the reports that my husband is sinking rapidly. He is not, nor is he recovering rapidly. It will be a long, hard fight to win, but I feel he will eventually." A few days later, Mathewson's doctor, E. N. Packard, told a *Times* reporter, "Reports circulated that he has surrendered to despondency and abandoned his fight are entirely unfounded. . . . I want to assure Mathewson's countless friends that he is doing as well as can be expected under the circumstances."

Despite these comments, the rumors continued. In early January 1921, Dr. Packard contacted journalists to deny reports that Mathewson had died, and said that he was improving slightly and "fighting like he did in the old days when he pitched for the Giants."

Mathewson, Jane and Christy Jr. were living in the Santanoni, an upscale apartment building on Church Street in Saranac Lake. Built in 1913, the Santanoni was home to tuberculosis patients with too much money to be admitted to the sanitarium. The building featured a common dining room where residents who were strong enough came for their meals. Those who were too ill, such as Mathewson, had their meals delivered from the establishment's kitchen.

Mathewson later said that the first months were the hardest. "You get into a very peculiar frame of mind," he said. "To your own surprise you find the tears roll down your cheeks."

Jane, too, found those times particularly difficult. She had been told that Christy had no chance and would soon die. She busied herself nursing him, which she said was the easiest part for her. "You see, they gave me no encouragement. But there was so much to be done that there was little time for brooding."

As part of his treatment, Mathewson slept on a cure porch, even when the temperature fell to thirty or forty below zero. He later said that he found the cold particularly hard to endure because he had lost so much weight, dropping from 185 to 150. The "absolute rest" that was the foundation of his care meant staying in bed and moving no part of his body except his lower arm.

By February 1921, he was making progress. He wrote to a friend in the Giants organization, "I will surely beat this game, but it will take twelve months longer to do it. I sit up in a chair an hour or so nearly every day and am getting stronger." The Mathewsons allowed a reporter to visit, although Jane did all the talking because Christy was too weak to speak. "He has been extremely nervous and impatient lately," she said. "I think it comes from reading about the ball clubs going south. You know, this is the first time in twenty-one years that he has not gone with them. He broke down and cried bitterly. I never saw him do that before."

Also in February, he received word from Washington that he would be paid $95 a month for total disability "resulting from injury incurred in the line of duty." The poison gas and the influenza he suffered from in France could not be proved to be connected to the tuberculosis, but they were judged significant enough to justify the disability payments.

In August, a Chicago jury acquitted the White Sox players accused of rigging the 1919 Series. Mathewson felt strong enough to talk to a reporter, who asked what he thought of White Sox manager Kid Gleason—who was not involved in the fix—remaining friendly with the players who had cost him the championship. Mathewson said: "There is such a thing as condemning the act of these men and still forgiving the individuals. I don't think Gleason and the rest of the White Sox wanted to see their former comrades sent to the peniten-tiary for from two to five years. They would not have been human if they did." Concerning ballplayers' performance in general, although perhaps thinking of Hal Chase and the Black Sox, Mathewson said, "A baseball player who does not do his best every day—the best he can possibly do that day—should be disciplined, and if he persists should be released."

By the end of August, Mathewson was growing still stronger. He had gained some weight and was taken on drives in the country. Delighted to be outdoors, he enjoyed the scenery and told Jane, "It is a good old world." On August 30, he appeared in the village for the first time, driven by Jane to a barber shop. His haircut merited a story in the *New York Times*.

On September 30, the game between the Giants and the Boston Braves at the Polo Grounds was dedicated to Mathewson, with the proceeds going to help out with his medical expenses. The program book was filled with tributes from sportswriters. Hugh Fullerton wrote: "If America has produced a finer example of athlete, he will be hard to find. Matty means a lot more to us than baseball. He stands out as the idol and the ideal of the national sport. He is typical of the best that baseball stands for, and in the minds of the younger gener-ation Matty means baseball of the cleanest, highest type. We owe him a lot; he played hard, he played fair, and asked no odds and expected no favors. He took the fortunes of the game as they came—and he smiled whether he won or lost."

The regular game was preceded by an exhibition game between the current Giants and players from the pennant-winning Giants teams on which Mathewson played. Then there was an auction of autographed baseballs, the prize among these being one signed by Mathewson, President Warren Harding, Vice President Calvin Coolidge, Babe Ruth, Walter Johnson, Ty Cobb, George M. Cohan, and other players and celebrities. The winning bid was $450 by a man who took the ball but never sent in his check.

After one inning of the Giants-Braves game, rain poured down and the game was cancelled. But sportswriter Fred Lieb, who was chairman of the event, had paid $2,500 for a $25,000 insurance policy to protect against a rainout. So that amount was added to the gate receipts and auction proceeds, and Mathewson received a check for $54,500. In his thank-you letter to Giants executive Francis McQuade, Mathewson said, "I am flat on my back and can't go out and spend it," but added that he intended to invest the money in securities that "will net me around $3,000 a year." He also wrote: "I notice in the papers that I am about to cash in. Well, don't you believe it. I am going to get well enough to come down to the Polo Grounds and slap you on the back while we watch the Giants win another pennant."

Mathewson's optimism was starting to appear well-founded. By early 1922, he was increasingly visible around Saranac Lake. He threw out the first ball at one of the village team's games, and he worked with the local American Legion post to secure financial assistance for the approximately 650 World War I veterans who were being treated for tuberculosis in the area.

He was willing to use his celebrity to draw attention to the disease and its victims, and to inspire other patients. His physician, E. N.

Packard, said: "We are all happy for his cure, for it will act as an incentive to others. Here in Saranac, Matty's remarkable recovery has been responsible for more patients getting up from sick-beds and out in the open than all the medicine which we could ever prescribe. When a particularly stubborn case is encountered, we tell them about Matty."

But beyond the public's view, Mathewson endured difficult times. He was undergoing pneumothorax treatment, which involved pumping air into the pleural cavity between the lung and the chest wall. This would cause the lung to collapse, with the pumped-in air occupying space to prevent the lung from inflating and doing its normal work. With enforced rest imposed on the tubercular lung, it could have a better opportunity to heal. Because the air leaks out, the pumping had to be done weekly, and sometimes even more often.

In late 1922, Mathewson suddenly developed excruciating pain in his side. His temperature climbed, and his doctor found that fluid forming in the pleural cavity had become infected. This fluid had to be drained and replaced with glycerine and formaldehyde. The tract where the hypodermic needle had entered his side became a large, open sore, and if he moved in his bed infected fluid would drain out. His temperature and his pain kept increasing. One night in particular, Jane and the doctor did not believe that he would live until morning. Mathewson later recalled, "When you get that bad, you don't care anymore."

Somehow, he made it through the crisis. As his health slowly improved, so did his optimism. Whenever he slipped toward despair, he said, he would tell himself, " 'You're not playing a very good game today—that's no way to play the game.' I reminded myself and reminded myself. It's like a couple of baseball players. Maybe they've struck out three times in a pinch that day, and everything looks black. Then they go along the street and see some fellow with his legs off and with his hat in his hand. And they'll say, 'Well, what are we kick-

ing about?' That was just the way with me. There is just one way to
get yourself out of a discouraged frame of mind—just recall someone
who is sick and in the same trouble, only a whole lot worse."

As his condition improved, he went for longer drives in the country
and found a new hobby: identifying wildflowers. At first, he said, "when
I saw a daisy, I knew it was a daisy, and when I saw a clover, I knew it
was a clover, but that was all." Soon, with the aid of several books, he
was identifying everything. He was an inveterate list maker, and he
wrote out a list of sixty-one different flowers that he had spotted. His
favorite was the blue gentian. He also kept a day-by-day record of the
flowers he saw, beginning in June 1922 and continuing into August.
The list was on page after page of note paper that he taped together into
one continuous sheet that became several feet long.

He also went hunting, in a limited fashion. Jane recalled, "We
would drive along the mountain roads in an automobile. We watched
the side of the road closely. If signs of a covey of quail or grouse were
observed, the car would stop and Christy, with his shotgun, would
step on the ground on the side of the car away from the quail. Then
he would slowly walk toward the birds until the covey flushed. He
never shot one except upon the wing. He often secured the bag limit."

Also among his projects was developing a new baseball board
game called Big Six—his old nickname—which he touted at every
opportunity. A good way to get him to agree to being photographed
was to suggest that he hold a Big Six box when the picture was taken.

In August—more than two years after he had arrived in Saranac
Lake—Mathewson took his first extended trip. He traveled by car to
Factoryville for a visit with his parents to mark his forty-second birthday. He tossed a baseball with some local boys, and spent much of his
time playing checkers with his father. He told a reporter, "I am almost
well," and when asked for a message to schoolboys, he said: "By all
means, play ball. It brings you to rub elbows with the world. It will
teach you much, if you will but learn." He warned that "conceit and

overconfidence are the worst enemies a ballplayer has," and added: "Do not let them turn your head. Be humble and gentle and kind."

As his health improved, Mathewson grew increasingly restless and thought more and more about baseball. He knew that managing again was out of the question; the stress would quickly wear him down. Coaching with the Giants would involve too much travel. Jane wanted him to keep rooted at Saranac Lake, where his recovery had taken place.

What seemed a perfect opportunity suddenly appeared, emerging from a dinner party at New York's Lambs Club. In the dinner four-some were John McGraw; entertainer George M. Cohan; Harry Stevens, who ran the food concessions at many sports venues; and Judge Emil Fuchs, the Giants' attorney. McGraw spotted Boston Braves owner George Washington Grant and told Cohan: "You always wanted your own baseball team. Grant's is for sale." Cohan declined, saying he'd stick to his own brand of showbiz. Then McGraw turned to Fuchs. "Why don't you buy it?" Fuchs surprised his companions by promptly replying, "Sure." Then he attached a condition: Christy Mathewson had to help run the team.

McGraw had kept in touch with Mathewson by telephone, and knowing of his desire to get back into the game, he urged Fuchs to call Mathewson in Saranac Lake.

Mathewson was receptive to becoming the team's president. Jane was opposed. But the next day, Mathewson told Fuchs, "I would rather spend another two or three years in the only vocation I know than to linger many years up in Saranac Lake."

Mathewson meant that after two or three years he would retire. But Dr. Edward Baldwin, one of Trudeau's associates, believed the risk was great and told Mathewson: "You'll last about two years if you go back to baseball."

Jane later said, "I think it was the worst possible decision." They were having a house built in Saranac Lake, and she hoped that they could remain there. Christy could spend time outdoors, hunting and fishing, while staying in the curative environment with plenty of tuberculosis specialists on hand. That, however, was too logical an argument to overcome the allure of baseball.

Mathewson told the press that he thought the Braves, who had lost a hundred games in 1922, could be developed into a decent team. He noted that he had seen his first big league game in Boston in 1899, when he was pitching for Taunton. "I sat behind the screen at the old Walpole Street grounds and watched Cy Young and Kid Nichols in a brilliant pitching duel. And I paid seventy-five cents for that seat where I could watch those masters perform."

Mathewson's true return to baseball took place in April 1923 when the Braves played the Giants on opening day at the Polo Grounds. Writing in the *New York Tribune*, Grantland Rice described the moment: "A king walked out of the shadows of the past into the brilliant spring sunshine of the Polo Grounds yesterday as 30,000 loyal subjects paid him the tribute of a roaring acclaim that no crowned monarch could ever know. . . . More than the might of his arm and the stoutness of his heart, there was the clean sincerity of the true sportsman to bring him the devotion of the crowd. No name in baseball has ever meant the same as that of Christy Mathewson. . . . He was the link to yesterday, a memory of young Aprils that have been lost in the quick rush of the years, a grip upon old times and old occasions. . . . As Matty and McGraw shook hands, the present had completely surrendered to the past."

Although his energy was limited, Mathewson performed a team president's standard duties, such as sending a season pass to the White House. President Calvin Coolidge, who was familiar with the team from his days as governor of Massachusetts, acknowledged the Braves' difficulties, saying that he hoped to "someday see your team win."

Coolidge had become president in 1923 on the death of Warren Harding and had inherited a government weakened by corruption. Some of Harding's cronies had decided to enrich themselves through misuse of government resources, such as the oil reserves at Teapot Dome in Wyoming. Graft also flourished in the Veterans Bureau and other government agencies.

While Congress investigated, a booming economy—climbing toward the heights from which it would fall in 1929—kept most Americans happy. Coolidge could safely embrace the status quo and let the country take care of itself, with minimal interference from government.

The easy road beckoned. Woodrow Wilson's idealism and the challenges that accompanied it belonged to the past. Now there were profits to be made and good times to be enjoyed.

The Coolidge prosperity, however, was partly built on flaws in the American character. Greed was good, and gangsters such as Al Capone saw themselves as the entrepreneurs of the Roaring Twenties.

One of the shrewdest observers of endangered American character was novelist Sinclair Lewis. In *Main Street* and *Babbitt*, wrote historian Frederick Lewis Allen, Lewis "revealed the ugliness of the American small town, the cultural poverty of its life, the tyranny of its mass prejudices, and the blatant vulgarity and insularity of the booster."

Like Booth Tarkington's *The Turmoil* from the prewar years, Lewis's books were extremely popular because of their stories and their moral lessons. If the values of Midwestern towns could be perverted, what would become of the country? Were any traditions safe? Despite Judge Landis's zeal, even baseball, soiled by the Black Sox, was in questionable health.

Enter Babe Ruth. He had been in the majors since 1914, making his reputation first as a dominating pitcher for the Boston Red Sox. His best year on the mound was 1916, when he went 23-12 with a 1.75 earned run average.

He didn't emerge as the game's biggest star until Boston sold him to the New York Yankees after the 1919 season. He promptly hit an astounding 54 home runs, changing baseball into a game in which power could take precedence over finesse. Facing Ruth and the generations of power hitters that followed, a pitcher was often "in a pinch" because of the damage one swing of the bat could do.

He was a very different kind of celebrity than Mathewson had been. Ruth always seemed comfortable as a public figure, but he had no interest in being seen as a model of virtue and sportsmanship. He liked liquor and women—plenty of both—and made no secret of it. The public loved him, vicariously thrilled by his exploits on the field and off.

A visitor to Mathewson at Saranac Lake tried to get him to pass judgment on Ruth and his apparent lack of self-control. But Mathewson wouldn't bite. "Ruth is what he is," he said. "It is his temperament that makes him so valuable to baseball and so worthy of his salary. The mass of people on the bleachers care most for a man whom they can cheer today and jeer tomorrow, and Ruth fits into that picture."

Ruth dominated baseball news in the 1920s much as Mathewson had before him. As different as their personalities were, they had one important characteristic in common: their ability to expand the game's audience and make baseball an even more integral part of American life. In that sense, Ruth was Mathewson's successor.

While Ruth was swatting home runs, Mathewson was starting to rebuild the Braves. He told Fuchs, "If we want a first division club, we've got to pay major league salaries." They raised the team payroll from the $80,000 of 1922 to more than $200,000 in 1923. Mathewson also scrutinized the Braves' financial operations. His players had enjoyed generous expense accounts that they used to treat their friends to meals. When Mathewson cut the meal allowance back to four dollars a day, angry players decided that he was not one of them, but just another management tightwad.

Mathewson and Fuchs got along well. Among other aspects of

their relationship, they were formidable bridge partners. Mathewson tried to attend all the Braves' home games, but he also spent a lot of time in Saranac Lake, where Christy Jr. was finishing up at the local high school and where the new house was finally ready.

Just down the street from the Trudeau Sanatorium, the house at the intersection of Old Military Road and Park Avenue looks today much as it did in 1924, when the Mathewsons moved in. It stands on a hill looking down on the rest of its triangular lot, appearing, to the imaginative, like a pitcher on the mound. Inside it is spacious but not grand, with the comfortable living room and dining room comple-mented by glassed-in porches. Upstairs, two of the bedrooms have doors onto open decks where Mathewson could rest in the fresh air.

He and Jane recognized the value of making Saranac Lake their home, as opposed to moving to Boston or returning to New York. He told a reporter that he would not permit any article about him to be published that proclaimed "How I Beat TB." He said: "If I err, I pre-fer to do it on the side of caution. If I had the use of both lungs, I would feel that I was well, but one is still collapsed and I realize that I am not a cured case." About his preference for staying in Saranac Lake, he said: "One trouble with people who come back among their friends is that the friends do not understand tuberculosis. If a man doesn't immediately go in for dinners, theater, and other social activity, his friends may very well become his enemies if they urge him on to activ-ity and try to convince him that he is perfectly well. That doesn't do. He needs to remind himself that he is not as good as he was."

He also emphasized the importance of being near the sanatorium and other tuberculosis patients. "In a sanatorium, or in a cure cot-tage, you're in touch with other people in the same condition. You hear how they are getting on . . . and you commiserate with each other in ways that don't drag you down." He acknowledged the importance of resignation, "not passive resignation, but intelligent submission, and a calm assurance that your misfortune is only temporary. You can't help what you can't help. If anyone had told me when I was first taken sick that I would be in bed for fifteen months, I would have answered, 'Carry me right over to the graveyard.'" But now, he said, he was willing and able to continue the fight.

His efforts with the Braves did not produce immediate results. In 1923, the team again lost a hundred games, although they emerged from the league cellar, climbing over prostrate Philadelphia, which lost 104. Mathewson's old teammate Rube Marquard had come to the Braves and was nearing the end of his career, going 11-14 in 1923. In 1924, Boston lost a hundred once more and fell back into last place. Not until 1925 did they finally show some life, finishing fifth with a 70-83 record.

As 1925 began, Mathewson was working hard. He wrote to the other National League team presidents asking for financial help for Duke Farrell, a former catcher and scout who was dying of stomach cancer. He sent a letter to his old boss Garry Herrmann in Cincinnati turning down a proposed trade. And he joined the team in Florida for spring training.

He and Jane stayed at the new Soreno Hotel in St. Petersburg, a three hundred–room establishment that was the city's first million-dollar hotel. They relaxed, with just a bit of work thrown in. He liked the sunshine and the casual pleasures of baseball in the spring. Even more, he relished the memories of years past, when he and John McGraw and the rest of the Giants were tuning up to pursue another championship.

All was well. Then he caught a cold.

That's all it was—a cold that would have been just a minor annoyance to almost anyone. But for a tuberculosis patient, it was more than that.

They went home to Saranac Lake, to their nice new house in the town that had provided miracles in the past. He went to bed to shake the cold, but it wouldn't be shaken. Then his temperature began to rise.

In the attic of their house, a list was found. On Soreno Hotel note paper, in what appears to be Mathewson's handwriting, is a tempera-ture chart. Page after page, day after day, from April 11 until September 29, is the neatly quantified record of Mathewson's health. On some days he was particularly feverish, and the readings were over 100. For September 29, in large letters is written, "Normal."

But the recovery was illusory. During the next week, he faded. As his lungs failed, Christy told Jane, "Go into the other room and have a good cry. But don't make it a long one. This can't be helped."

They planned the funeral and spent quiet moments together.

And then he died.

Afterword

He traveled once more to Lewisburg, to the parlor of Jane's family home on Market Street.

W. O. McGeehan wrote in the New York *Herald Tribune*, "As he lay there in the bower of flowers, clad in one of those plain brown suits he used to wear, he looked, as his pastor said, like a sun-crowned man."

The funeral was simple: a prayer by the president of Bucknell, a Gospel reading and a few words from Reverend Frank Everitt, pastor of the Lewisburg Presbyterian Church, and a hymn. Reverend Everitt said: "His standards were not weakened by the stress and toil of the athletic field. Christy Mathewson lived on the athletic field to establish those standards. He did more than any one man to stabilize the moral standards of modern sport."

On that crisp, windy Saturday afternoon, the pallbearers, including John McGraw and several of Christy's boyhood friends from Factoryville, escorted the body along streets lined with flags at half-staff.

In the cemetery adjacent to the Bucknell campus, the gravestone does not stand out from others. It is relatively small and just says "Mathewson." In front of it are markers for Christy, Jane and Christy Jr. A more substantial monument is nearby—a gateway on the campus, built two years after his death. The inscription reads: "Athlete, soldier, gentleman. He was one of the greatest figures in competitive sport of all time."

Tributes appeared in newspapers throughout the country. The Bucknell paper said, "He became the standard by which other players were judged, with the remarkable result that baseball was elevated unbelievably in tone." The New York *World* said: "Christy Mathewson was one of those rare figures in sport who transform it . . . into the glamorous thing we would wish it to be. . . . He was a vindication of our love for sport."

The leading sportswriters also had their say. Grantland Rice wrote: "He was something more than a great pitcher. He was one of those rare characters who appeal to millions through a magnetic personality attached to clean honesty and undying loyalty to a cause." W. O. McGeehan offered more praise, but made it clear that he was not proposing sainthood: "Let none of us insult the memory of Christy Mathewson by making of him one of those sanctimonious and insufferably perfect heroes. . . . Christy Mathewson took his drinks with men. He delighted in a game of poker. He swore a good full-mouthed oath when he felt the need of it. There is nothing that makes me angrier than the perpetuation of the legend that he was . . . a sort of prig."

Perhaps the most heartfelt comments came from Mathewson's friend and mentor, John McGraw. "Mathewson's real greatness to the game lay in examples he set for young fellows and the impression he left on the minds of the public. . . . Christy Mathewson had a natural dignity that did much to raise the morals of his teammates. He influenced them to look upon baseball as an honorable profession—one that required skill and constant appreciation. . . . I do not expect to see the like of Mathewson again, but I do know that the example he set and the imprint he left on the sport that he loved and honored will remain long after I have gone. Mathewson was my close friend. His passing is one of the greatest sorrows of my life. God rest his soul."

More tributes were paid, and life went on.

Christy Jr. graduated from Bucknell in 1927 with a degree in electrical engineering. His father had never pressured him to pursue a baseball career, and both parents encouraged him to follow his own interests. Christy Jr. saw the wisdom in that. "They would always point to me as my great dad's son," he said, "and besides, you don't know how awful a baseball player I am."

His greatest love was flying. After briefly working for General Electric, he joined the Army Air Corps. By 1932 he was in Hangchow, China, serving as an instructor at the Central Aviation School, part of a quiet American effort to build up China's fledgling air force.

In Hangchow on Christmas Eve, 1932, Christy married Peggy Phillips of Philadelphia. Escorted by Jane Mathewson, Peggy had traveled nine thousand miles for the wedding. Two weeks after the ceremony, the newlyweds went to Shanghai for a weekend with friends. They planned to fly back to Hangchow, which would be Peggy's first flight with her husband as pilot. They were using a twin-engine Sikorsky amphibian that belonged to the Chinese finance minister.

Less than a minute after takeoff, the plane crashed into the bank of the Huangpu River. As he was pulled from the wreckage with two broken arms and a shattered leg, Christy said, "Look after my wife." But Peggy was dead.

Jane, who was waiting for the couple at their Hangchow home, rushed to the Shanghai hospital. Christy would remain there for several months, and his leg had to be amputated.

Jane stayed in China for almost a year, until Christy was well enough to come home. He returned to Saranac Lake, where he lived with his mother, regained full use of his arms, and mastered his prosthetic leg. In 1941, he was working in Washington, D.C., as an aeronautical engineer for a War Department committee that was planning for America's likely entry into the war. After Pearl Harbor, Christy was recommissioned as a captain in the Air Corps and became the command liaison officer of the Chinese Training Program, based in Phoenix. Continuing the work he had begun in China, he supervised the instruction of Chinese pilots, who were then sent home to fight the Japanese. Rising to the rank of lieutenant colonel, he also served in Europe with the Air Transport Command.

He married a woman from Saranac Lake in 1936, and they were divorced in 1945. Shortly thereafter he married a woman he had met in London. There were no children.

He retired from the military and settled in the outskirts of San Antonio, Texas. At his home there in August 1950, he was installing an electric dishwasher when he touched off a gas explosion that blew through the house. Severely burned over most of his body, he died a few hours later. He was forty-three.

Jane had continued to live in Saranac Lake, in the house she and Christy had built in 1924. She had invested wisely in the stock market after her husband's death, and she lived comfortably. She indulged her fondness for jewelry and furs, but in other ways she was frugal. She never owned a television or an air conditioner, and she always made her own soap.

She followed baseball from a distance. The president of the National League sent her a pass each year, but she never used it. "I just can't bring myself to attend a game at the Polo Grounds," she said in 1938. "If I looked out on the field at the pitching box where Christy stood so often, the memories would be too poignant." At Blanche McGraw's urging, she did attend a game in Saranac Lake when Jeff Tesrau, who had been Christy's teammate on the Giants, brought an amateur team from Vermont to play the locals.

After Christy Jr.'s death, she moved back to Lewisburg, to the house where Christy had courted her, where they had been married, and where Christy's coffin had rested before his funeral. She led a quiet life, joining a sewing bee with old friends and regularly going to church. She made a substantial donation to Phi Gamma Delta, her husband's fraternity at Bucknell, to be spent on a new kitchen, and she joined the boys for dinner there several times each year.

She became close friends with Betty Cook, also from an established Lewisburg family. Fifty years Jane's junior, Betty became a
surrogate granddaughter, and encouraged Jane to reestablish her
baseball ties. Jane began going to Cooperstown each year for the
National Baseball Hall of Fame induction ceremonies. Christy had
been one of the five original members of the Hall (along with Ty
Cobb, Walter Johnson, Babe Ruth and Honus Wagner), and Jane
was always among the most honored guests at the induction of new
members.

She cherished Christy's reputation as both a splendid athlete and
role model, but she did her best to deflate unrealistic portrayals. She
said that he "never tried to pass as a paragon of virtue," and when she
was asked if it was true that he never smoked, drank or cursed, she
winked and said, "You don't think I'd marry such a prude, do you?"

Her last visit to Cooperstown was in 1966, when she rose and
took a bow before the ceremony honoring that year's inductees, Ted
Williams and Casey Stengel. The following May, she threw out the
first pitch at a new softball field in Lewisburg.

A few days later she became ill and entered the hospital. On May
29, she died. She was eighty-seven.

"He was a gentleman." You read that time and again in the contemporary appraisals of Christy Mathewson. Even before people
described his wonderful athletic skills, they talked about his
demeanor and his integrity.

He transformed baseball by his presence, which incorporated a
dignity and moral stature the game had not known. Adhering to his
own standards of sportsmanship, he didn't quarrel with umpires, he
didn't taunt opponents, and he didn't throw at batters. Instead, he
rose above the rowdy, loutish status quo and lifted baseball with him.

The public responded. Professional baseball attracted more fans
and individual players became role models. Mathewson inspired chil-

dren to play baseball and to do so with the "combination of bodily vigor and moral quality" that Theodore Roosevelt prescribed.

Mathewson also epitomized the maturation of American character. By 1900, the country was preparing itself for a more significant place in the world. Roosevelt's "strenuous life" was the training regimen for this new role, and it too had a moral as well as a physical dimension. In pursuing that life, Mathewson did more than play a game; he showed how the game could bring out the best in those who dedicated themselves to it. This grasping of excellence was an essential step not just for ballplayers, but also for a nation that was entering "the American century."

A few years later, during Woodrow Wilson's presidency, Mathewson moved beyond setting standards of on-field performance. He embraced Wilson's "high code of honor" and tried to police his sport. But just as Wilson failed to win political support for his vision of a postwar world order, Mathewson was unable to convince baseball's leadership to forcefully respond to threats to the game. Both men knew their failures would lead to greater problems. When he returned home from the war, Mathewson was angered but not surprised by the corruption of the 1919 World Series.

Even the Black Sox scandal did not destroy the optimism and determination that were integral elements of Mathewson's character. During his struggle against tuberculosis, he once again found himself viewed as a symbol of hope and strength. When he appeared to have won his fight, Americans applauded the triumph of virtue.

And when people learned that Mathewson had finally lost his battle, they saluted his courage and mourned. Those who had cheered him for so many years knew he had done his best. They understood that even a great champion could be vulnerable and even in the glittering America of the 1920s life could be cruelly unfair.

In victory Mathewson was admirable. In defeat he was magnificent.

Acknowledgments

Writing this book has taken me on a fascinating trip through an important era in American history and has reinforced my lifelong love of baseball. I appreciate the assistance provided by the A. Bartlett Giamatti Research Center of the National Baseball Hall of Fame and Museum; the Special Collections/University Archives of the Bertrand Library at Bucknell University; the athletic department and library of Keystone College; the Adirondack Research Center of the Saranac Lake Free Library; and the Society for American Baseball Research.

Those who offered advice, help and support include Norm Brauer, Bill Burdick, Claudette Burke, Jerry and Barbara Connolly, Betty Cook, Susan Day, Joe Drape, Doris Dysinger, Eric Enders, Eddie Frierson, Penney Gentile, Jeremy Jones, Rachel Kempner, Tom Knock, Linda Menck, Rick and Gail Meyer, Charlie and Deborah North, Gabriel Schechter, Michele Douglas Tucker, Sheila Webb, Tim Wiles, and Terry Wise.

At Four Walls Eight Windows, Jofie Ferrari-Adler has been an enthusiastic editor and friend as this book has taken shape.

Special thanks to my agent Robbie Anna Hare for her extraordinary persistence. A book that mixes baseball biography and cultural history is not an easy sell in today's publishing world, but Robbie kept the faith and kept working.

My wife, Christine Wicker, may be bemused by baseball, but she never wavered in her affectionate support of this book and its author.

Notes

CHAPTER 2

Page

21. **Just up the street**: Jeff Kisseloff, *You Must Remember This* (Baltimore: Johns Hopkins University Press, 1989), 255.

21. **The *New York Herald* reported**: Mark Sullivan, *The Turn of the Century* (New York: Charles Scribner's Sone, 1936), 514, 529.

22. **The Giants were run by Andrew Freedman**: Charles Alexander, *Our Game* (New York: Henry Holt, 1991), 69-70.

27. **"The biggest move we made"**: John J. McGraw, *My Thirty Years in Baseball* (Lincoln, NE: University of Nebraska Press, 1995), 138.

27. **"Aggressiveness is the main thing"**: McGraw, *My Thirty Years in Baseball*, 66, 13, 175.

27. **"It was an education to play under John McGraw"**: Lawrence S. Ritter, *The Glory of Their Times* (New York: William Morrow, 1992), 91.

28. **"According to Mr. McGraw"**: Ritter, *The Glory of Their Times*, 174.

28. **"Because he knew how to handle men"**: Ritter, *The Glory of Their Times*, 131.

28. **As yet he had not begun to study pitching**: McGraw, *My Thirty Years in Baseball*, 139, 141.

29. A "distinctly gory" loss: Edmund Morris, *The Rise of Theodore Roosevelt* (New York: Coward, McCann and Geoghegan, 1979), 113.

30. "Don't any of you realize?": Henry F. Pringle, *Theodore Roosevelt* (New York: Harcourt, Brace and World, 1956), 156.

31. While he was en route: William Allen White, *The Autobiography* (New York: Macmillan, 1946), 336.

32. The number of cars on U.S. roads: Sullivan, *The Turn of the Century*, 494, 369.

33. Newspapers had noted: Mark Sullivan, *America Finding Herself* (New York: Scribner's, 1971), 227.

34. "It seems to me": Steven A. Riess, *Touching Base: Professional Baseball and American Culture in the Progressive Era* (Urbana, IL: University of Illinois, 1999), 179.

35. Mathewson was part of the first wave: Riess, *Touching Base*, 284, n. 75.

36. "Athletic proficiency is a mighty good servant": Jean Paterson Kerr, *A Bully Father* (New York: Random House, 1995), 127.

36. Echoing Roosevelt was editor and social critic Herbert Croly: Herbert Croly, *The Promise of American Life* (New York: Macmillan, 1910), 452, 454.

37. "I like to see Quentin practicing baseball": Kerr, *A Bully Father*, 234.

37. "You must always remember": Edmund Morris, *Theodore Rex* (New York: Random House, 2001), 81.

37. "Three new throws": Kerr, *A Bully Father*, 149.

38. "When all is said and done": Mario R. DiNunzio (ed.), *Theodore Roosevelt: An American Mind* (New York: St. Martin's, 1994), 127-132.

38. "The effective control of vulgarity": Bill James, *Bill James' Historical Baseball Abstract* (New York: Villard, 1986), 61.

38. A number of factors beyond baseball itself: Riess, *Touching Base*, 12.

39. "The stock market didn't close": Ritter, *The Glory of Their Times*, 176.

39. The lower-class fans: Riess, *Touching Base*, 38.

39. In 1897, the Washington Senators: Riess, *Touching Base*, 34, 36.

40. "Every father of a normal boy": William Randolph Hearst, "Parents, Attention: Why All American Boys Should Play Base Ball," *Sporting Life*, May 2, 1903, 1.

CHAPTER 3

Page

43. "We sat in the lobby of the De Soto Hotel": Mrs. John J. McGraw, *The Real McGraw* (New York: David McKay Company, 1953), 191.

44. "The streets were mostly empty and quiet": Kisseloff, *You Must Remember This*, 155.

44. "Together we made a study": McGraw, *My Thirty Years in Baseball*, 140.

45. "The brain of McGraw": Christy Mathewson, *Pitching in a Pinch* (New York: Grosset and Dunlap, 1912), 127.

46. "I seek boys who can think": McGraw, *My Thirty Years in Baseball*, 142.

48. "It is mathematically poor dope": F. C. Lane, *Batting* (Cleveland: SABR, 2001), 135.

51. "You may not realize what that affidavit": W. J. MacBeth, "In All Fairness," *New York Tribune*, September 26, 1921, 11.

53. "It is in the pinch": Mathewson, *Pitching in a Pinch*, 57.

53. In 1902, immigration: Sullivan, *The Turn of the Century*, 573.

54. During the century's first decade: Warren Zimmermann, *First Great Triumph* (New York: Farrar, Straus and Giroux, 2002), 455.

54. "New York city is still amply clad": R. W. B. Lewis and Nancy Lewis (eds.), *The Letters of Edith Wharton* (New York: Scribners, 1988), 97.

55. **"Mathewson to boy and man"**: F. L. Brunner, "Hero Worship on the Diamond," *Baseball Magazine*, April 1914, 50.

56. **In an article for *Baseball Magazine***: Mathewson, "Baseball in Its Worthier Aspects," 19, 21.

57. **"When you see him behind a roll-top"**: Homer Croy, "Christy in the Swivel Chair," *Baseball Magazine*, March 1909, 8.

58. **One morning in Pittsburgh**: Jack Sher, "Christy Mathewson—The Immortal 'Big Six,'" *Sport*, October 1949, 60.

59. **"I was at most Matty's editor"**: Roger Kahn, *The Head Game* (San Diego: Harcourt, 2000), 97.

60. **"Nobody has ever done my work for me so far"**: Sher, "Christy Mathewson," 63.

61. **Mathewson's books**: Andy McCue, *Baseball by the Books* (Dubuque, IA: Wm. C. Brown, 1991), 27.

CHAPTER 4

Page

69. **Well-known athletes could make**: Larry D. Mansch, *Rube Marquard* (Jefferson, NC: McFarland, 1998), 95.

69. **"Where else can people who don't know anything"**: Robert W. Snyder, *The Voice of the City* (New York: Oxford, 1989), 46.

70. **A few theaters featured Dutch boxer**: Joe Laurie, Jr., *Vaudeville* (New York: Henry Holt, 1953), 124.

72. **Victoria Theater**: Laurie, *Vaudeville*, 381.

73. **Hammerstein arranged to have Machnow arrested**: Laurie, *Vaudeville*, 387-391.

73. **On hot summer days**: Snyder, *The Voice of the City*, 90.

73. **Lavishly designed restaurants**: Lewis A. Erenberg, *Steppin' Out* (Westport, CT: Greenwood, 1981), 41, 51, 146.

75. **Kane filed an alienation of affection suit**: Mansch, *Rube Marquard*, 124, 126.

75. **"Marquard hasn't done himself or the New York club"**: Mansch, *Rube Marquard*, 125.

76. **"Conventions which had been respected"**: Mark Sullivan, *The War Begins* (New York: Scribner's, 1936), 165.

76. **It was, however, unlike urban centers**: Sullivan, *The War Begins*, 200, 202, 204.

76. **What few extra hours they had**: Riess, *Touching Base*, 47.

76. **"The greatest single force"**: Riess, *Touching Base*, 29.

77. **"Fairness, cheerfulness"**: Harold Seymour, *Baseball: The People's Game* (New York: Oxford, 1990), 57.

77. **"Attended by thousands of men and boys"**: Jane Addams, *The Spirit of Youth and the City Streets* (New York: Macmillan, 1909), 95.

77. **"The enormous crowd of cheering men"**: Addams, *The Spirit of Youth*, 96.

78. **"Baseball fostered social integration"**: Steven A. Riess, *Sport in Industrial America 1850-1920* (Wheeling, IL: Harlan Davidson, 1995), 165.

79. **President William Howard Taft**: Arthur Susskind, Jr., "Taft Rated Top Fan Among Presidents," *Sporting News*, April 11, 1962, 3.

80. **"To Walter Johnson"**: Jack Kavanagh, *Walter Johnson* (South Bend, IN: Diamond Communications, 1995), 32.

80. **"To get much more than amiably tolerant"**: Sullivan, *The War Begins*, 307.

81. **"When I hear someone say"**: Sullivan, *The War Begins*, 460.

CHAPTER 5

Page

89. **"The crowd opened up like the Red Sea"**: Albert G. Spalding, *America's National Game* (Lincoln, NE: University of Nebraska, 1992), 441.

90. **He was estimated to have preached**: Lyle W. Dorsett, *Billy Sunday and the Redemption of Urban America* (Grand Rapids, MI: Eerdmans, 1991), 93.

90. **Sunday jokingly remarked**: Dorsett, *Billy Sunday*, 95.

91. "**There is not a more corrupting thing**": Roger A. Bruns, *Preacher: Billy Sunday and Big-time American Evangelism* (New York: Norton, 1992), 142.

92. "**The boys of the past generation**": Spalding, *America's National Game*, 542.

92. "**The Giants blew up**": Christy Mathewson, "Why We Lost Three World Championships," *Everybody's Magazine*, October 1914, 538, 539, 540, 544.

94. "**In my many years of following the World Series**": Fred Lieb, *Baseball As I Have Known It* (New York: Coward, McCann &Geoghegan, 1977), 93-95.

95. **The Giants lived at Marlin's Arlington Hotel**: Frank Graham, *McGraw of the Giants* (New York: Putnam's, 1944), 42.

99. "**Of course, I realize I'm through**": Ritter, *The Glory of Their Times*, 226.

101. **Wilson was editor of the campus newspaper**: Henry Wilkinson Bragdon, *Woodrow Wilson: The Academic Years* (Cambridge, MA: Belknap/Harvard, 1967), 35, 38.

102. **In a pregame ceremony**: Kavanagh, *Walter Johnson*, 127.

103. "**His basic, lifelong faith**": John Morton Blum, *Woodrow Wilson and the Politics of Morality* (Boston: Little, Brown, 1956), 197.

103. **Wilson "resembled other American Protestants"**: John Milton Cooper, Jr., *The Warrior and the Priest* (Cambridge, MA: Belknap/Harvard, 1983), 19.

103. "**If under Roosevelt social reform**": Goldman, *Rendezvous with Destiny*, 169.

105. "**Skillfully took his country**": Philip Bobbitt, *The Shield of Achilles* (New York: Knopf, 2002), 362.

105. "**Like Wilson, most Americans**": Blum, *Woodrow Wilson and the Politics of Morality*, 109.

CHAPTER 6

Page

107. **"He was a pinhead"**: Kahn, *The Head Game*, 107.

109. **Like Mark Twain's *Tom Sawyer***: James Woodress, *Booth Tarkington* (Philadelphia: Lippincott, 1955), 178.

112. **Hobey Baker was admired**: John Davies, *The Legend of Hobey Baker* (Boston: Little, Brown, 1966), 82, 74.

113. **"He was playing the puck, not me"**: Davies, *The Legend of Hobey Baker*, 50, 51.

113. **After graduating from Princeton**: Davies, *The Legend of Hobey Baker*, 80.

113. **"You handle your machine instinctively"**: Davies, *The Legend of Hobey Baker*, 96.

115. **"I want to tell you fellows"**: Fred Lieb, *Baseball as I Have Known It* (New York: Coward, McCann and Geoghegan, 1977), 98.

116. **"His neatest trick"**: Lieb, *Baseball as I Have Known It*, 100.

117. **Mathewson was dismayed**: Charles C. Alexander, *John McGraw* (Lincoln, NE: University of Nebraska Press, 1988), 207.

120. **"The testimony showed that Chase"**: Martin Donell Kohout, *Hal Chase* (Jefferson, NC: McFarland, 2001), 208.

CHAPTER 7

Page

125. **Mathewson was part of a massive infusion**: David M. Kennedy, *Over Here: The First World War and American Society* (New York: Oxford, 1980), 177, 205.

125. **The American troops had been told**: Paul Fussell, *The Great War and Modern Memory* (New York: Oxford, 1975), 13, 16.

126. **"Nowhere among Germany's remaining resources"**: John Keegan, *The First World War* (New York: Vintage, 1998), 412.

128. **Ty Cobb, however, told of a training exercise**: Al Stump, *Cobb* (Chapel Hill, NC: Algonquin, 1994), 276.

130. **These 550 Americans found themselves**: Robert H. Zieger, *America's Great War* (Lanham, MD: Rowman and Littlefield, 2000), 106.

137. **His first soldierly act**: Arthur Mizener, *The Far Side of Paradise* (Boston: Houghton Mifflin, 1965), 70.

138. **"America was going on the greatest, gaudiest spree"**: F. Scott Fitzgerald, *The Crack Up* (New York: New Directions, 1956), 87.

139. **They wouldn't speak to each other**: Kohout, *Hal Chase*, 216.

CHAPTER 8

Page

144. **"A man standing on a chair"**: James Crusinberry, "A Newsman's Biggest Story," *Sports Illustrated*, September 17, 1956, 69.

146. **"The biggest first inning you ever saw"**: Eliot Asinof, *Eight Men Out* (New York: Henry Holt, 1963), 116.

147. **He had thrown fifteen pitches, all fastballs**: Asinof, *Eight Men Out*, 118.

147. **"There will be a great deal written"**: Dean A. Sullivan (ed.), *Middle Innings: A Documentary History of Baseball, 1900-1948* (Lincoln, NE: University of Nebraska, 1998), 90.

148. **Moran turned to pitcher Hod Eller**: Ritter, *The Glory of Their Times*, 219.

149. **"Most costly error"**: J. W. Sehorn, "Hal Chase Replays His 'Costliest Error'," *Sporting News*, April 23, 1947.

150. **"Can't we get a postponement of the case"**: Bruce Watson, "The Judge Who Ruled Baseball," *Smithsonian*, October 2000, 122.

150. **"No intelligent man doubts"**: David Pietrusza, *Judge and Jury: The Life and Times of Judge Kenesaw Mountain Landis* (South Bend, IN: Diamond Communications, 1998), 312.

151. **"Birds of a feather flock together"**: Pietrusza, *Judge and Jury*, 187, 192.

151. **He declared war on gamblers**: Watson, "The Judge Who Ruled Baseball," 127.

152. "**Every lawful and ethical means**": A Bartlett Giamatti, *A Great and Glorious Game* (Chapel Hill, NC: Algonquin Books, 1998), 120-121.

153. "**They deserve it**": Sher, "Christy Mathewson," 62.

153. **When the Giants were in Chicago**: Helena Lorenz Williams, "The Come-Back of Christy Mathewson," *Journal of the Outdoor Life*, February 1924, 76.

153. **In the United States**: Victoria E. Rinehart, *Portrait of Healing: Curing in the Woods* (Utica, NY: North Country Books, 2002), xvii.

154. "**Papers and books can be left**": Alfred L. Donaldson, *A History of the Adirondacks* (Port Washington, NY: Ira J. Friedman, 1963), vol. 1, 241.

155. "**Factory girls**": Rinehart, *Portrait of Healing*, 20.

155. **Using the tubercle bacillus**: Rinehart, *Portrait of Healing*, 24.

155. **Sanitarium patients were charged**: Rinehart, *Portrait of Healing*, 50.

155. **Trudeau told of finding Stevenson**: Donaldson, *A History of the Adirondacks*, vol. 1, 279.

156. "**Trudeau was all winter**": Donaldson, *A History of the Adirondacks*, vol. 1, 286.

156. **The popularity of the sanitarium method**: Rinehart, *Portrait of Healing*, 40.

156. "**Cure cottages**": Philip L. Gallos, *Cure Cottages of Saranac Lake* (Saranac Lake, NY: Historic Saranac Lake, 1985), xx.

156. **One study of the sanitarium's former patients**: Rinehart, *Portrait of Healing*, 51.

159. "**You see, they gave me**": Williams, "The Come-Back of Christy Mathewson," 77.

162. " '**You're not playing a very good game'** ": Williams, "The Come-Back of Christy Mathewson," 79-81.

163. "**We would drive along**": Robert Taylor, *Saranac: America's Magic Mountain* (Boston: Houghton Mifflin, 1986), 141.

164. "You always wanted your own baseball team": Harold Kaese, *The Boston Braves* (New York: Putnam's, 1948), 190.

164. "I would rather spend another two or three years": Robert S. Fuchs and Wayne Soini, *Judge Fuchs and the Boston Braves* (Jefferson, NC: McFarland, 1998), 24.

164. "You'll last about two years": Taylor, *Saranac*, 143.

166. Lewis "revealed the ugliness": Allen, *Only Yesterday*, 229.

167. "If we want a first division club": Fuchs and Soini, *Judge Fuchs*, 42.

167. When Mathewson cut the meal allowance: Kaese, *The Boston Braves*, 199.

168. If I err: Williams, "The Come-Back of Christy Mathewson," 82.

Selected Bibliography

BOOKS

Addams, Jane. *The Spirit of Youth and the City Streets*. New York: Macmillan, 1909.

Alexander, Charles C. *John McGraw*. Lincoln, NE: Bison, 1995.

———. *Our Game*. New York: Henry Holt, 1991.

Asinof, Eliot. *Eight Men Out*. New York: Henry Holt, 1963.

Blum, John Morton. *Woodrow Wilson and the Politics of Morality*. Boston: Little, Brown, 1956.

Bobbitt, Philip. *The Shield of Achilles*. New York: Knopf, 2002.

Bragdon, Henry Wilkinson. *Woodrow Wilson: The Academic Years*. Cambridge, MA: Belknap/Harvard, 1967.

Bruns, Roger A. *Preacher: Billy Sunday and Big-time American Evangelism*. New York: W. W. Norton, 1992.

Chadwick, Henry (ed.). *Spalding's Official Baseball Guide 1902*. New York: American Sports Publishing, 1902.

Chadwick, Lester. *Baseball Joe at Yale*. New York: Cupples and Leon, 1913.

———. *Baseball Joe on the Giants*. New York: Cupples and Leon, 1916.

Cooper, John Milton, Jr. *The Warrior and the Priest*. Cambridge, MA: Belknap/Harvard, 1983.

Croly, Herbert. *The Promise of American Life*. New York: Macmillan, 1910.

Davies, John. *The Legend of Hobey Baker*. Boston: Little, Brown, 1966.

Day, Donald (ed.). *Woodrow Wilson's Own Story*. Boston: Little, Brown, 1952.

DiNunzio, Mario R. (ed.). *Theodore Roosevelt: An American Mind*. New York: St. Martin's, 1994.

Donaldson, Alfred L. *A History of the Adirondacks*. Port Washington, NY: Ira J. Friedman, 1963.

Dorsett, Lyle W. *Billy Sunday and the Redemption of Urban America*. Grand Rapids, MI: Eerdmans, 1991.

Erenberg, Lewis A. *Steppin' Out: New York Nightlife and the Transformation of American Culture 1890-1930*. Westport, CT: Greenwood, 1981.

Fitzgerald, F. Scott. *The Crack Up*. New York: New Directions, 1956.

————. *This Side of Paradise*. New York: Scribner's, 1920.

Fuchs, Robert S. and Wayne Soini. *Judge Fuchs and the Boston Braves*. Jefferson, NC: McFarland, 1998.

Fussell, Paul. *The Great War and Modern Memory*. New York: Oxford, 1975.

Gallos, Philip L. *Cure Cottages of Saranac Lake*. Saranac Lake, NY: Historic Saranac Lake, 1985.

Giamatti, A. Bartlett. *A Great and Glorious Game*. Chapel Hill, NC: Algonquin, 1998.

Goldman, Eric F. *Rendezvous With Destiny*. New York: Vintage, 1956.

Graham, Frank. *McGraw of the Giants*. New York: Putnam's, 1944.

James, Bill. *Bill James' Historical Baseball Abstract*. New York: Villard, 1986.

Kaese, Harold. *The Boston Braves*. New York: Putnam's, 1948.

Kahn, Roger. *The Head Game*. San Diego: Harcourt, 2000.

Kavanagh, Jack. *Walter Johnson*. South Bend, IN: Diamond Communications, 1995.

Keegan, John. *The First World War*. New York: Vintage, 1998.

Kennedy, David M. *Over Here: The First World War and American Society*. New York: Oxford University Press, 1980.

Kerr, Jean Paterson. *A Bully Father: Theodore Roosevelt's Letters to His Children*. New York: Random House, 1995.

Kisseloff, Jeff. *You Must Remember This*. Baltimore: Johns Hopkins University Press, 1989.

Kohout, Martin Donell. *Hal Chase*. Jefferson, NC: McFarland, 2001.

Lane, F. C. *Batting*. Cleveland: SABR, 2001.

Laurie, Joe Jr. *Vaudeville*. New York: Henry Holt, 1953.

Lewis, R. W. B. and Nancy Lewis (eds.). *The Letters of Edith Wharton*. New York: Scribners, 1988.

Lieb, Fred. *Baseball As I Have Known It*. New York: Coward McCann and Geoghegan, 1977.

Mansch, Larry D. *Rube Marquard*. Jefferson, NC: McFarland, 1998.

Mathewson, Christy. *Catcher Craig*. New York: Dodd, Mead, 1915.

————. *First Base Faulkner*. New York: Dodd, Mead, 1916.

————. *Pitcher Pollock*. New York: Dodd, Mead, 1914.

————. *Pitching in a Pinch*. New York: Dodd, Mead, 1912.

————. *Second Base Sloan*. New York: Dodd, Mead, 1917.

————. *Won in the Ninth*. New York: R. J. Bodmer, 1910.

Mayer, Ronald A. *Christy Mathewson*. Jefferson, NC: McFarland, 1993.

McCue, Andy. *Baseball by the Books*. Dubuque, IA: Wm. C. Brown, 1991.

McGraw, Blanche. *The Real McGraw*. New York: David McKay, 1953.

McGraw, John J. *My Thirty Years in Baseball*. Lincoln, NE: University of Nebraska Press, 1995.

Mizener, Arthur. *The Far Side of Paradise*. Boston: Houghton Mifflin, 1965.

Morris, Edmund. *The Rise of Theodore Roosevelt*. New York: Coward, McCann and Geoghegan, 1979.

———. *Theodore Rex*. New York: Random House, 2001.

Pietrusza, David. *Judge and Jury: The Life and Times of Judge Kenesaw Mountain Landis*. South Bend, IN: Diamond Communications, 1998.

Pringle, Henry F. *Theodore Roosevelt*. New York: Harcourt, Brace and World, 1956.

Riess, Steven A. *Sport in Industrial America 1850-1920*. Wheeling, IL: Harlan Davidson, 1995.

———. *Touching Base: Professional Baseball and American Culture in the Progressive Era*. Urbana, IL: University of Illinois, 1999.

Rinehart, Victoria E. *Portrait of Healing: Curing in the Woods*. Utica, NY: North Country Books, 2002.

Ritter, Lawrence S. *The Glory of Their Times*. New York: William Morrow, 1984.

Robinson, Ray. *Matty*. New York: Oxford, 1993.

Roosevelt, Theodore. *American Ideals*. Charles Scribner's Sons, 1926.

———. *Autobiography*. New York: Charles Scribner's Sons, 1926.

———. *The Strenuous Life*. New York: Charles Scribner's Sons, 1926.

Seymour, Harold. *Baseball: The People's Game*. New York: Oxford, 1990.

Snyder, Robert W. *The Voice of the City: Vaudeville and Popular Culture in New York*. New York: Oxford, 1989.

Spalding, Albert G. *America's National Game*. Lincoln, NE: University of Nebraska, 1992.

Stump, Al. *Cobb*. Chapel Hill, NC: Algonquin, 1994.

Sullivan, Dean A. (ed.). *Middle Innings: A Documentary History of Baseball, 1900-1948*. Lincoln, NE: University of Nebraska, 1998.

Sullivan, Mark. *Our Times*. New York: Scribner's, 1936.

Tarkington, Booth. *Penrod*, in John Beecroft (ed.), *The Gentleman from Indianapolis*. Garden City, NY: Doubleday, 1957.

———. *Seventeen*. Garden City, NY: Doubleday, Page, 1922.

———. *The Turmoil*. Garden City, NY: Doubleday, Page, 1922.

Taylor, Robert. *Saranac: America's Magic Mountain*. Boston: Houghton Mifflin, 1986.

Voight, David Q. *America Through Baseball*. Chicago: Nelson-Hall, 1976.

Wheeler, John. *I've Got News for You*. New York: E. P. Dutton, 1961.

White, William Allen. *The Autobiography*. New York: Macmillan, 1946.

Woodress, James. *Booth Tarkington*. Philadelphia: Lippincott, 1955.

Zieger, Robert H. *America's Great War*. Lanham, MD: Rowman and Littlefield, 2000.

Zimmermann, Warren. *First Great Triumph*. New York: Farrar, Straus and Giroux, 2002.

ARTICLES AND OTHER DOCUMENTS

Brunner, F. L. "Hero Worship on the Diamond." *Baseball Magazine*, April 1914.

Croy, Homer. "Christy in the Swivel Chair." *Baseball Magazine*, March 1909.

Crusinberry, James. "A Newsman's Biggest Story." *Sports Illustrated*, September 17, 1956.

Hearst, William Randolph. "Parents, Attention: Why All American Boys Should Play Baseball." *Sporting Life*, May 2, 1903.

Lane, F. C. "The Secret of Christy Mathewson's Success." *Baseball Magazine*, October 1916, 65-70.

Lardner, Ring W. "Matty." *American Magazine*, August 1915, 26-29.

Mathewson, Christy. "Baseball in Its Worthier Aspect." *Baseball Magazine*, March 1909, 19-21.

———. "My Life So Far." *Baseball Magazine*, December 1914, 53-66.

———. "Why We Lost Three World's Championships." *Everybody's Magazine*, October 1914, 537-547.

Sehorn, J. W. "Hal Chase Replays His 'Costliest Error.'" *Sporting News*, April 23, 1947.

Sher, Jack. "Christy Mathewson - The Immortal 'Big Six.'" *Sport*, October 1949.

Susskind, Arthur, Jr. "Taft Rated Top Fan Among Presidents." *Sporting News*, April 11, 1962.

Watson, Bruce. "The Judge Who Ruled Baseball." *Smithsonian*, October 2000.

Williams, Helena Lorenz. "The Come-Back of Christy Mathewson." *Journal of the Outdoor Life*, February 1924.

Index